CAR DRIVING IN
2 WEEKS

In the same series are several companion books. We recommend specially A. Tom Topper's LEARNING TO DRIVE IN PICTURES, which brings a different, picture-packed approach to the subject. The same author's VERY ADVANCED DRIVING, drives on, for all who wish to strive for greater safety on our roads.

HIGHWAY CODE – QUESTIONS AND ANSWERS provides a most enjoyable quiz-type review of the Highway Code in *terms of the sorts of questions examiners ask.*

TEACH YOUR SON OR DAUGHTER TO DRIVE, by David Hough, is aimed at the amateur instructor, whether parent, relative, or interested friend. Learner and teacher use the book together. The 10 lessons provide an in-depth analysis of the Highway Code to match with progressive driving practice. The book sorts out what to teach, in what order, and HOW. Early lessons secure safe car handling without any need for dual control, or for plunging into thick traffic too soon. Later lessons graduate increased exposure to traffic, so as to maintain confidence as experience is gained. At the core of the book are the key lifetime driving skills which will keep your pupil safe beyond the Driving Test.

Every car cubby-hole should carry a copy of EMER-GENCY CAR REPAIRS, a get-you-started and/or get-you-home goldmine of breakdown knowledge, suitable even if you have never before looked under a bonnet.

Lawrence Nathan's

CAR DRIVING IN 2 WEEKS

Lawrence Nathan was formerly a Branch Manager with the British School of Motoring Ltd. and later founded the Right Way Schools of Motoring; he was also a recipient of the Certificate of the Royal Society for the Prevention of Accidents and a registered driving instructor with the R.A.C. Diploma.

Revised, extended and re-written by

ANDREW M. HUNT

PAPERFRONTS
ELLIOT RIGHT WAY BOOKS
KINGSWOOD, SURREY, U.K.

CONTENTS

PAGE

Introduction   7

PART ONE: THE LEARNER'S SECRET

1. Before you start   11
2. Clutch Control for a Smooth Take-off   14
3. Stopping   28
4. Steering   39
5. Changing Gear   42

PART TWO: DRIVING THE CAR

6. Driving along   51
7. Right of Way and Traffic Regulations   58
8. Signalling   68
9. Left and Right Turns   80
10. Traffic Lights and Roundabouts   105
11. Overtaking   117
12. Manoeuvres, Reversing, Parking   130
13. Automatic Transmission   144

PART THREE: THE DRIVING TEST

14. You are on Test   148
15. Chief Reasons for Test Failure   151
16. Some Questions Commonly Asked by Examiners   153
17. Summing up for Learners   169

PART FOUR: AFTER YOUR TEST

18. Motorways   171
19. The More Advanced Driver   178

INDEX   189

LIST OF ILLUSTRATIONS

		Page
1.	Typical gear positions	16
2.	How the clutch pedal works	20
3.	Steering wheel hold	39
4.	Failing to straighten up quickly enough after a right turn	41
5.	Gear changes in relation to speed	43
6.	Correct travelling position on a road with only one lane each way	52
7.	A left filter green arrow	54
8.	Right of way when there is a parked vehicle	59
9.	Unseen arm turn signal	69
10.	When to signal	71
11.	Correct arm signals	73
12.	Passing a parked vehicle	76
13.	A very common accident	79
14.	Correct path for a left turn on to a major road	84
15.	Danger of an overtaking vehicle when turning left	86
16.	Swinging out at left turn. **WRONG**	87
17.	Mounting the pavement by mistake	88
18.	Correct position and path for turning right, off a major road	91
19.	Rights of way when turning right	92
20.	Cutting a right hand corner. **WRONG**	94
21.	Bad turn caused by creeping forward	95
22.	Hatch road markings	96
23.	**CORRECT** way for two drivers to turn right at crossroads	98
24.	A congested crossroads	99
25.	Passing in front (nearside-to-nearside) when turning right at crossroads	100
26.	Traffic lights at roadworks	107
27.	"Mini" roundabout sign	108
28.	A busy urban roundabout	113
29.	An unusual roundabout	115
30.	You are clear to overtake the lorry	119
31.	Mirrors and door pillars blind spots	121
32.	A false sense of security	123
33.	Fatal errors	125
34.	Steering in reverse	131
35.	Three-point-turn front wheel positions	133
36.	Reversing into a narrow street to the "difficult" side	137
37.	Parking between cars at the kerbside	143

INTRODUCTION

The title *Car Driving In 2 Weeks* does not mean that anyone of seventeen or over can magically pass their Test in so short a time, although with the benefit of practically full-time effort, it has often been done. Most people take months longer gaining regular practice. Nevertheless we believe this book can vastly increase its readers' chances, not just in passing the Test but in building themselves a lifetime record of accident-free driving pleasure.

There are no special accolades for speed of learning. Rushing the job beyond your own capability, is a mistake which frequently leads to failure of a Test taken too early, as well as to a very natural blow to confidence. The sensible choice, of taking as long as you individually need to become really good, is the best recipe for a first-time pass.

The author has been personally responsible for thousands of learners passing their driving tests; add on the several readers of each copy of this book sold to date, and the number of drivers he has helped must run into millions.

You will read here of the faults and remedies which Test examiners look for. If you put into practice the instructions in this book, you should pass. You must have a commonsense attitude, associated with good road sense, and remember never to insist on having "right-of-way" while driving.

There are no insurmountable difficulties, nor is the road to success too severe, but you have to drive well because the examiner has to be convinced that you are competent to drive safely in all circumstances.

Ninety per cent of Test failures are due to inexperience in traffic. However, it is not sufficient just to have had a lot of experience, if that experience includes the learning of mistakes. Some mistakes show an examiner that a candidate has not got a clue. This book enables you not only to find the "clue", but to solve the enigma: *How to pass the Driving Test.*

Car Driving In 2 Weeks supplements the teaching which whoever is instructing you must provide in the car. All the background information you need to pass your Test is here, sufficient indeed, if the cost of driving school lessons is beyond your means, for you to learn with a friend or relative as instructor.

Some years ago, much lobbying by the driving school industry, won the passing of the law in the U.K. which makes it illegal to charge for giving driving lessons unless you are professionally qualified by passing a government instructors' test. The law stopped short of preventing any other driver holding a full licence from acting as unpaid instructor, and quite rightly. It is not widely enough known that, despite all their "qualifications", statistics show that people taught by professional instructors fair little better than those who are taught by others with good driving records. The first-time pass rate of our Driving Test remains under 50%. It has hovered just under half for a very long time, and since long before the driving instruction law was passed. Combine this with the fact that 9 out of 10 learners obtain *some* professional instruction, and you can see that the standard of teaching which professionals provide is by no means automatically better than most good drivers are able to achieve.

The publishers of this book regard the present high Test failure rate as stemming principally from candidates' lack of sufficient driving practice, the one thing vested driving school interest would have them denied – except via school lessons at huge cost. We trust that Parliament will always uphold the sturdy individualism for which our country is renowned, and never allow such self-seeking lobbying to result in banishing people's right to pass on their driving skills.

We have some superb drivers, and the hard-won experience at their fingertips is too precious to be wasted.

In saying all this we do not wish to demean the talent and hard work of good professional driving instructors. Local individual reputations (your best guide) confirm how excellent many of these men and women are at their job. So much so, that most learners who know of a good instructor will probably want to combine some school lessons with other practice.

Nevertheless, this book strongly recommends, if you are able to have a good teaching/learning rapport with a friend or relative with a long safe-driving record, that you go out for as much practice as he or she can manage time to give you. However, avoid too long spells at the wheel in one session; you tire more easily to begin with than you may believe, and a tired driver is a danger on the road.

Over-tiredness is probably the most culpable hidden factor which our huge road accident statistics will never prove. Remember that. And do not drive if you are unwell.

About 5,000 people per year die on British roads. Hundreds of thousands are injured, with about one fifth of these being serious cases. Appalling though these figures are, we nevertheless have one of the lowest road-accident death rates in Europe. However, despite that, we continue to be among the worst for our record of killing and maiming young children of school age. Why? is a question we must never forget when at the wheel.

During your life you have one chance in three of being injured if you are only an *average* driver. Our aim in publishing this book, and we hope your objective in reading it, is to help you reduce this risk. Over one and a quarter million successful Driving-Test candidates have relied on *Car Driving In 2 Weeks,* so its techniques are well proven. The skills and sound driving philosophy put forward should become your guardian, and not just for the Test. After you pass, remember that learning goes on for the rest of your driving life.

Part 1 of this book explains how to control a car and get it to move or stop.

Part 2 teaches general driving around and about and how to carry out various manoeuvres, both for the Driving Test and for everyday use.

Part 3 describes the Test and the standards which must be met to satisfy an examiner.

Part 4 shows how you can improve your driving after passing the Test. Amongst the many things covered, it deals with skids and it takes in the use of motorways, on which you are not allowed to drive as a learner.

Beyond your Test pass we wish you a lifetime of good, safe, happy driving.

The Publishers.

PART ONE

THE LEARNER'S SECRET

1
BEFORE YOU START

I begin with general information which must seep into your consciousness from the moment you apply for your provisional licence through your local post office. (You have to wait until the licence arrives before you can drive.) Never again dare you be a wide-asleep passenger! You must develop a safe driver's thinking.

As driver it will be you who must ALWAYS look at the (road) wheels prior to taking the (steering) wheel, to make sure that you have not got a flat tyre. Before you split your sides with laughter at this 'ALWAYS' suggestion, I can assure you it is an essential habit and that it provides a consistent reminder to watch your tyres' condition. Tyre law, rightly, has become increasingly stringent, holding the driver responsible and with severe penalties. Tyre dealers can advise on the latest detailed regulations but in outline: (a) *any* bald patches render a tyre illegal to use, (b) *more* than 1mm of tread (expected to rise shortly to harmonise with other countries in the E.C.) must show all round a tyre, and for not less than three-quarters of the way across at any point, (c) bulges or slits in *either* of the side walls of a tyre are illegal, (d) inner cords of a tyre exposed or affected by a deep cut are outlawed, (e) your tyres must be maintained at the correct pressure and (f) differently constructed tyres may not generally be fitted to one vehicle.

You should know that the tyre pressures and the engine oil and coolant levels, have all been checked within the last week, or lesser time if more than 1,000 miles have been covered. If any of these are low, it can result in serious damage or lead to an accident. To comply with the Vital Driver's Check-List which I come to in a moment, another valuable weekly check, is to test and clean all your outside lights front and back and make sure the windscreen washer reservoir(s) (front, and back if fitted) is/are topped up (adding an ice inhibitor in winter). As driver you are responsible for the safe mechanical condition of the car. At first your instructor will have to advise of any faults in the performance of the car's steering, engine or brakes; later, with experience of how they and other major items like the speedometer (which must, by law, be operational) and the battery should be working, it will be up to you to make sure everything is up to scratch. Note that a defective tyre, for example, might also nullify your insurance cover, placing you at risk of losing everything you own, in the event of a major claim against you.

Vital Driver's Check-List

Whenever you take the wheel you must know that:

1. **All doors are properly closed.** Check before you get in. Double check in your wing mirrors.

2. **The driver's seat is locked in position** (for it to slide back as you tried to brake could be fatal). When the seat is suitably adjusted for you, your elbows and knees will be about half bent. From this position your reactions to steering and brakes will be at their most effective. Adjust it so that you can sit relaxed but sufficiently upright to command a full view, as much over the ground close to the bonnet as into the far distance, and for you to be at the same time within comfortable reach of all the major controls. If the steering wheel position is adjustable, that must be locked securely too.

3. **Seat belts are done up.** By law (apart from a very few obscure exceptions) seat belts must be worn by everyone in a front seat. Rear seat belts should also be worn. Children – who mostly travel in the back – suffer horrendous injuries in accidents where they have not been properly secured in seats.

You must also know that:

1. **Driving mirrors are clean and adjusted** to give you the fullest view. The interior mirror surround should "match" the rear window outline as closely as possible. Each side mirror should capture the view alongside the car; as a setting guideline you should be just able to "sight" the car's waistline towards the back.

2. **All windows are clean,** inside and out. (Apart from it being a little-known offence to have dirty windows, I believe they cause many more accidents than people realise. One greasy thumb-print can make a lethal blind spot. Sparkling clean

windows raise morale and help you open your eyes; a murky view makes you less alert, all round!)

3. **Windscreen wipers and washers all work effectively** (another legal requirement).

4. **All exterior lights work** and are clean, for full lightpower. Headlights must be properly adjusted to light the maximum correct field of view when dipped – without danger of dazzling others. (Note: convictions for failed lights can carry licence penalty points.)

5. **Your horn works** (it must, by law).

6. **Any load being carried is safely stowed.** Anything carried on a roof-rack must be properly tied so that it cannot slide in any direction. (Check strapping at every wayside stop you make.)

Always complete your checks as soon as you have the engine running (details shortly) with:

1. Will I need petrol? (The gauge only stops you running out *if* you habitually read it and you know how to quantify that reading in available miles! Looking every time you start helps the habit take hold.)

2. Are any dashboard lights warning me not to drive on? You should study the owner's handbook with your instructor, and make sure *you* understand the significance of all the major warning lights.

Despite the controversy which preceded the compulsory wearing of front seat belts in the U.K., early statistics have proven a large decrease in deaths and accident injuries. Legislation for the compulsory wearing of rear seat belts will, I hope, not be long delayed. Bodies being flung about in the car, and even arriving in the front from the back, are the ones to get hurt, and badly, where belts could prevent or lessen injury. Courts can rule that a car occupant who is not wearing a seat belt is partially to blame for the consequences of an accident; injury damages are then reduced accordingly.

No wonder the Highway Code urges you not to let children travel unrestricted in the luggage space of estate type cars. It advocates that they should travel in the rear seat, strapped in, even though it is not (yet) law, and with the door child-safety locks set. Under one year old, a rearward-facing infant safety seat is recommended, or else a fully-strapped-in carry cot with a secure cover so baby cannot be ejected; up to 4 or 5 years, or until too big, a child seat with straps should be used, and, thereafter, a child safety-harness, or the adult seat belt combined with an approved secure booster cushion. A child belted-up in the front with a booster cushion is safer than one sitting in the back unrestrained. In law, the driver is responsible for a child under 14 in the front being strapped in – babies in an infant safety seat, and over-one-year-olds by a method matching age and size as above.

Never wear a heavy coat which restricts movement. Never drive in "wellies" (green, or any other colour...), or heavy boots. They can slip off the accelerator, or jam under the brake pedal. Wed mud on your shoes is lethal. Wipe it off; never be too lazy to do so.

The law states that, as a learner, you must have a provisional licence, signed by you and in date, and that regulation-size "L" plates must be clearly displayed on the car front and back – without obstructing the windows.

Make sure the insurance policy specifically covers you as a learner driver, and that whoever is instructing you is also covered in that respect under the policy.

Examiners do routinely check a number of the items mentioned in this chapter. Where they notice anything amiss they can refuse to complete your Test.

2

CLUTCH CONTROL FOR A SMOOTH TAKE-OFF

Your first step, *before* starting the engine with the ignition key/switch, is to familiarise yourself with handling all the other basic controls and switches **without having to look down.** You are not ready for anything else until you can find everything quickly, without your eyes needing to leave the road ahead. As will be discussed in this chapter, your hand must be able on its own and without fail, to seek out and use the gear lever or handbrake; your feet must be at ease finding the right pedals (for which see below). With regard to the switches, it is essential that you are able to work the flashing indicators, all the lights (including the headlight dipswitch and the headlight flasher), and to operate the wipers and washer(s), and the heater and de-mister controls too, without having to *look* for any of them.

Step two, *before* attempting to drive to any destination, must be initial mastery, on an open piece of ground or in a *very quiet* road, of the steering, brakes, clutch and gears. **N.B.** The remaining chapters in Part One of this book concentrate on correctly integrating the use of all these controls. You need to read on and absorb everything in them before you first take the wheel to try what you have learned. You also need to preview Part 2, Chapters 6-10, so that the basic rules of the road will come to you naturally from the outset. The Highway Code must, at the same time, be studied in detail too.

If you have automatic transmission you will not need to worry about gear changes or using a clutch but you still need to begin in the same way in a quiet place to gain full command of your car before trying to cope with other traffic.

A Test pass with manual gears qualifies you to drive afterwards with automatic transmission. However, if you pass with automatic gears, you will be restricted to that type unless you pass again later with manual gears. You may be happy to accept that if you feel you are never going to need to drive a manual geared car, or if you prefer not to have to learn the co-ordination of clutch and gears right at the beginning, when there is so much else to be thinking about.

Using automatic transmission is explained in Chapter 13, and should be read by those concerned, in conjunction with the rest of Part One, which, while dealing with the smooth take-off using ordinary gears and clutch, sets out all the other things you have to know before your first mobile lesson!

During the initial familiarisation, *still before you start the engine for the first time,* get your instructor to show you how to use the ratchet release button on the handbrake. (Your foot should be on the footbrake to prevent the car running away!) The button has to be held in and the lever pulled *on* fractionally more than it was previously set, before you can let the brake off. It should also be held in for noiseless handbrake application. This saves wear on the ratchet teeth. He or she must help you to memorise how much strength you use to reach the full-on position of the lever, and to learn how to recognise, by feel, whether you have released it completely.

This is also the time to be getting the feel of where the three foot pedals are, and to practise selecting different gears without needing to look down at the lever. *Your eyes have to be on the road!* The clutch pedal, lefthandmost of the three, is operated with your left foot. The footbrake, in the middle, and the accelerator positioned to its right, are both used with your right foot (though never at the same time!). Each pedal is spring-loaded against foot pressure, coming back to its "off" position as you release it.

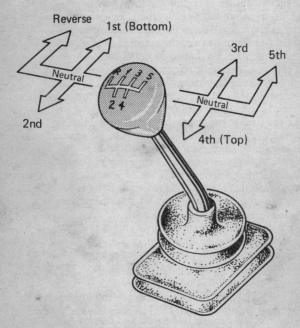

Fig. 1. Typical gear positions.

Press the clutch pedal down, so that the engine is disconnected from the gearbox (as will be explained), while you try the gear positions; otherwise the lever may be difficult to move. Notice how easily, when you are moving up or down the gears in sequence, the lever will almost self-seek its way towards the next gear. Your hand should guide the lever, never force it.

As engine speeds only have a narrow range, gears are essential so that the car can be moved off from rest, pick up speed easily, and be driven both slowly and quickly as occasion demands. The usual type of manual gearbox has a floor-mounted gear lever with six or seven positions. There are four or five forward gears, reverse and neutral. In neutral no gear is engaged; changing from any one gear to another always involves passing through neutral which acts as a buffer zone to help that transition. The other purpose for neutral will be explained when I come to the clutch. Fig. 1 shows the positions of the gear lever for a typical car. Whilst the forward gear positions and neutral are the same in most cars, reverse gear may be in various positions. The smooth take-off can be learned with 1st gear alone but you will soon be wanting to change gear on the move, and this "dry-run" practice will then stand you in good stead. You will need 2nd gear, for example, as soon as you are confident moving off in 1st and stopping again. 2nd lets you add a little speed whilst safe stopping ability is becoming second-nature. I will be dealing with the principles for changing gear in Chapter 5.

Starting The Engine
Before ever turning the key in the ignition switch to start the engine, a safety habit must be ingrained. It is physically to check that the handbrake is on and that the gear lever is in neutral *every* time, before you touch that key. Otherwise the car could lurch forward (or back ...) directly you operate the starter. There is a marginal saving of effort for the battery turning the engine over to start it, if you press the clutch pedal down while you operate the starter. But the fact that this separates the engine from the gearbox, as described shortly, must not be regarded as an excuse to skip your ingrained safety rule about checking, each and every time, that the handbrake is on and that you are out of gear. Examiners will not accept sloppy procedure. (A fault in the clutch, or your foot slipping off the pedal, could lead to an accident.)

Another essential before discovering how to use the starter itself is to understand the choke. This device enriches the fuel mixture to help start a cold engine. It may be automatic or manual. Your instructor can explain what type you have and how the makers state it works or should be used.

As the choke works in conjunction with the accelerator, care with that pedal is vital for easy engine starting. Pumping the pedal without thinking can flood the engine with fuel, making it difficult or impossible to start. Cars fitted with automatic chokes are sometimes especially sensitive in this respect.

Once an engine is hot you do not need choke to re-start it but the correct use of the accelerator can still be critical. Different engines have different requirements for starting when hot. Be sure you understand yours.

Manufacturers reckon a cold engine warms up most efficiently if the car is driven away directly the engine has overcome initial spluttering. Extra care must be exercised, however. Many serious accidents are caused by having the engine stall (cut out) at an awkward moment. An example would be when pulling out of a side street with what you thought was plenty of time. Too little manual choke may lead to an engine stall but so can too much, as, for example, if you forget to push off the choke control as soon as the engine runs well without it. You must learn exactly how much manual choke to use. Normally a choke should be pushed progressively right off within a couple of minutes' running. With an automatic choke the engine can still stall if you are unruly with the accelerator and flood the engine shortly after getting on the move. Again, if you have studied the manufacturer's instructions carefully, you should avoid trouble.

To start the engine, the normal arrangement in most cars is to turn the ignition key a little beyond the basic "on" position, against spring pressure. You then hear the starter spinning the engine. Instantly the engine starts – which you can also hear – you let go the key, which will then return itself to the basic ignition "on" position.

To stop the engine, you have to turn the key back further, to the "off" position.

Operate the starter in short bursts of five seconds or less. The engine should go at the first attempt but if not, brief tries, spaced out with a few seconds rest in between, give the battery a much better chance than a lengthy grinding effort; the latter is usually doomed to failure. Help the battery by switching off all electrical items, except sidelights where essential at night. If the engine will not start within about a dozen attempts, make sure you have not flooded it as discussed at the beginning of this section. The car handbook will describe what to do if you have, or where to look for other faults which may prevent starting. To go on trying remorselessly, without looking for the reason, will soon wreck your expensive battery. Your instructor should be able to tell you about any specific starting tips which help with the car you will drive.

After so much necessary theory the exciting first attempt at a smooth take-off still must await, yet, your grasp of the key component, the clutch.

The Clutch

The clutch is operated by the left pedal under the steering wheel as already noted. Its purpose is to ease the take-up of the load when you start off, and again, when you change from one gear to another.

The effect of the clutch is to disconnect the engine from the gearbox. You need to do this whenever you select and then engage a gear. When the clutch pedal is fully depressed, the engine is completely *dis*connected from the gearbox. When the clutch pedal is not depressed at all, the engine is fully connected *to* the gearbox. There is a point, in between, where the engine is only partly connected to the gearbox, and at that point the engine can be going fast, but the car (provided a gear has been selected) will only move slowly. What the beginner has to do, in order that he can move away slowly, is to discover that point. Normally, it is during the last three to five centimetres of clutch pedal release that the connection begins to take place.

The workings of the clutch consist of two tough flat plates, each having a span about the same as a pudding plate. They are positioned between the engine and the gearbox, as shown in fig. 2, opposing each other, rather like a pair of cymbals at the moment of striking. One plate is attached to the engine crankshaft, and rotates at whatever speed the engine happens to be running. The other is attached to the gearbox and thence connects, whenever a gear is engaged, through the transmission to drive the wheels.

When the clutch pedal is up fully, the two plates are locked together and turn together. The power of the engine – unless you are in neutral, out of gear – is transferred, via whatever gear is selected, out to drive the wheels.

When you press the clutch pedal down, the plates are drawn back from one another, disconnecting that power.

The point, already mentioned, of partial connection –where the engine plate begins to brush the gearbox plate, transmitting some power but without yet turning it fully as one – can be controlled with the clutch pedal. Doing so is known as *slipping the clutch* and is described in the next few pages.

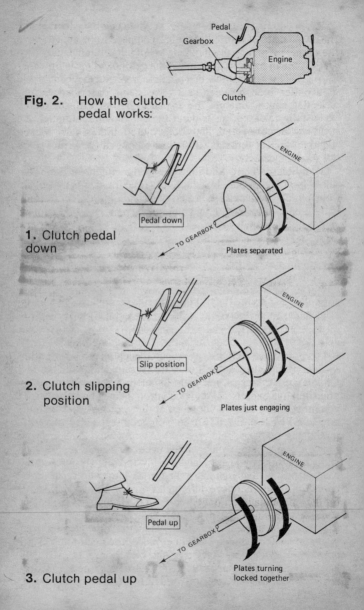

Fig. 2. How the clutch pedal works:

1. Clutch pedal down

Pedal down

TO GEARBOX

Plates separated

2. Clutch slipping position

Slip position

TO GEARBOX

Plates just engaging

3. Clutch pedal up

Pedal up

TO GEARBOX

Plates turning locked together

When you first start the engine, or when you have to wait in a traffic queue or at traffic lights etc., you need to be able to have the engine running without having to hold the clutch pedal down all the time in order to *dis*connect the gearbox. This is the other purpose of the neutral gearbox position, referred to when its role as a buffer zone between gears was being described earlier. Selecting neutral enables the engine to be run with the clutch pedal fully released but without the car moving: although the gearbox **is connected** and both clutch plates turn locked together, the car remains still because none of the actual gears are in engagement.

Many learners are told that to slip the clutch for a smooth take-off, a "slow" clutch pedal release is correct. This is not so; your clutch pedal release watch-word should be "controlled" rather than slow. Briefly, the method when moving off, involves releasing the clutch pedal *under control* up to the connection point, where it is held momentarily whilst you release the handbrake and make final safety checks; thereafter the remaining movement is *smoothly* released under control, when you are ready. The detailed steps I give shortly.

During gear changes on the move, further discussed in Chapter 5, all that is required for the release of the clutch pedal is to make it completely, in one continuous, swift, *smooth* movement, directly the next gear up or down has been selected.

I have stressed that you are going to need all the information in this book up to the end of Part One and to have studied Chapters 6-10 before you tackle your first smooth take-off – your first live exercise in clutch control. This is because before you move a car one jot, you must at the very least be aware of how to STEER it and STOP it! You need some idea of all the little things that can (but need not!) go wrong, and to understand how to change gear, which will be necessary virtually from the start. In addition, you are obliged in law to know the rules of the road. Study of these chapters and your Highway Code *must come first,* and, therefore, although I present the detailed steps for the smooth take-off now, I do so in the form of a convenient check-list to which you can return when you are ready.

I make the presumption that when the time comes your instructor will drive you to a quiet place, the need for which I have emphasised, and that he or she will choose an area with level ground and no parked cars or obstructions near to worry about. If you have to begin on a road rather than on open ground,

your instructor should stop the car a little further out from the
kerb than is normal for parking, so that you won't have to worry
about being too close to it.

When you finally swap places with your instructor, into the
driving seat for real, hold it! THINK! Have *you* run through the
Vital Driver's Check-List (page 12)? You are responsible –
every time *you* drive! What must *you* do before *you* start the
engine...? (See page 17.)

Smooth Take-Off From The Kerb

This smooth take-off check-list begins with the car on a *level*
place and with you ready, both hands on the steering wheel
(correctly positioned as per Chapter 4), *looking at where you
are about to go, not at the controls*. The handbrake is on, you
are in neutral, the engine is ticking over (your foot is off the
accelerator). If on open ground, you can imagine the line of a
kerb.

So, here you go! First time round, make sure the engine is
already fully warmed up and running evenly (which it should be
if your instructor has driven you to the quiet place chosen).

1. Press the clutch pedal well down with your left foot.
Keep it there.

2. Move the gear lever to **1st gear** position and bring your
hand back to the steering wheel.

3. Give gentle acceleration with your right foot on the
accelerator pedal. The sound of the engine should now be a little
more distinct. You have accelerated its "beat" from a "tick-
over" to just more than a fast idling speed, that is from just under
1,000 r.p.m. (revolutions per minute – if your car has a rev-
counter, you can check) to about 1,500 r.p.m. Maintain the
louder engine "rev" by keeping the accelerator pedal gently
squeezed down, but not too much.

4. Allow the clutch pedal to come up, under control. It will
be the last three to five centimetres of clutch pedal release that
count. *It is perfect control here, that determines whether you
achieve a smooth getaway, or a jumpy one.* If your heel will
reach the floor, where it can act as a pivot, you will find this a
great help. As the next Step is approached *under control*, the
point of partial connection which has already been described,
will be reached. You can recognise it, because the sound of the
engine quietens slightly.

**5. Stop releasing and hold the clutch pedal steady at this
partial connection point.** Don't alter your accelerator foot

position. Keep the engine "rev" exactly as set initially. You are now slipping the clutch. (The "screaming" extra engine revs you will often witness other learners produce at this point are *not* required.) Should you feel the car "rarin' to go", physically straining against the handbrake, lower the clutch pedal just enough to stop that happening but no more; that attempt by the car to creep against the handbrake only meant you had released the clutch pedal by a very small amount too much.

6. Release the handbrake. Keep both feet rock-steady 'til Step 7 in a moment. Return your handbrake hand to the steering wheel.

There is no rush to alter your feet positions now, because the car should stay still.

If it does start to move ahead slightly, then lower the clutch pedal a tiny fraction, just enough to stop that movement. Then hold the clutch pedal steady in that position. Remember, it is the clutch you finely adjust, *not* the accelerator. You keep that right where you set it in the first place. However, with a little practice, you will get the exact point to hold the clutch pedal right first shot, and avoid the need for any such fine adjustment.

There is now time for a final check all around that *it will be safe* to move the car. As well as checking all mirrors, this must include a look behind over your right shoulder, a look which, both for safety and because it is a Test requirement, must become an ingrained habit in your procedure for moving off from the kerb. It is also the time to give a moving off signal, for which see page 77. (Begin to incorporate the signal as soon as you become competent at the smooth take-off itself.)

Should it become obvious, just as you reach Step 6 and are slipping the clutch poised to go (which you will in Step 7), that you are going to have to wait for more than a few seconds (say for a child cyclist to pass), re-apply the handbrake and, at the same time, press the clutch pedal back down. You are then ready to return the clutch pedal to the partial connection point and take off the handbrake again, as soon as the cyclist has gone. By avoiding slipping the clutch any more than is strictly necessary, you help reduce wear on the clutch plates. If any longer delay looks likely to be involved, return the gear to neutral as well, and then release the clutch. Doing so saves unnecessary wear of the clutch thrust bearing whilst you await the chance to begin again.

7. Once safe to move, make sure you are now *looking ahead* again, and then *smoothly* **release the remaining upward**

movement of the clutch pedal.

This is all that is needed to get you away without any jerk. Do not jump off the clutch pedal. And do not change the accelerator yet. Control the release of the remaining movement of the clutch pedal as one continuous smooth operation.

If you hurry this final clutch release by mistake, quickly depress the pedal by just the amount you raised it, thus returning to the beginning of Step 6. You *can* recover and go on again from this stage but, if you need more time to collect thought, put the pedal fully down, apply the handbrake and return to neutral before starting again.

Once the car is moving away and the clutch pedal has been fully released, you can apply a gentle, firmer squeeze on the accelerator so that the car picks up speed.

Remember to steer along the left hand side of the road (or of the road you are visualising). There is no need to pull out fully while you still are only moving slowly; just drive straight ahead. This is why I have urged that your instructor should find a quiet place where there will be nothing in the way for you to have to steer round during this first time you take the wheel, and for him not to have parked too close to any real kerb. Later, Chapter 6 will explain how to move gradually out to an ideal travelling position.

8. After a few metres **STOP THE CAR** – as instructed in the next chapter (which I urged you to read before beginning at Step 1!).

You need lots of smooth take-off and stopping practice now, before adding gear changes, covering any great distance, or anything else. This will bring confidence in stopping, long before you ever exceed the speed available in 1st gear, a speed which can be fatal nevertheless.

Having completed Step 5, some drivers find they prefer to keep the handbrake on until after the safety checks and signal of Step 6, making its release the final item just prior to Step 7. There is nothing wrong in doing so, or switching to this method later on, but from a teaching beginners point of view, I have found this tends to lead to reliance on the handbrake to hold the car still, instead of developing 100% correct footwork. Then, later, when the stresses of other traffic intrude, the right way with the feet gets forgotten and all hell breaks loose! The key words for everything you do on Test are *under control.* The examiner will not be so concerned with which method you may have adopted with your instructor, as with the result – whether you always have your car *under control.*

Although I have taken you slowly through the **7** Steps of the smooth take-off, suggesting no rush, your aim by the time you begin general driving should be to be able to carry it out all-of-a-piece, subject only to the safety checks revealing a need to pause.

Driving along after the clutch pedal is fully up, rest your left foot comfortably away from the pedal (a little to the left is best, or raise your knee to let your foot come back towards you, or do a little of both). Avoid the common bad habit of driving along with your foot touching the clutch pedal, however lightly; this quickly causes excessive wear of the clutch thrust bearing. Never let either foot wander under the pedals. This could rob you of vital seconds in emergency braking. For the same reason keep clutter out of the driver's footwell too.

Note: In Step 1 of the smooth take-off I said press the clutch pedal "**well down**". In future, having now gained a feel for how far down in the pedal's range of movement the connection point comes, you only need to make sure you start with it below that point. There is no need to waste unnecessary energy going right to the floor with the pedal.

The Slightly More Advanced Driver

The "L" driver should appreciate that regrettably few experienced drivers show mercy to the learner who is taken amongst traffic too early. Suppose the "L" driver is held at a red light, first in the queue, when it changes. The beginner gets excited, or is too eager, and stalls. Then a selfish driver behind gets impatient and sounds his horn. This further excites the learner, who then goes to pieces. See what I mean? Do not panic; this is not the end of the world. Others can wait, or pass round you. First get your handbrake on; then collect thought calmly, secure in the knowedge that since you have already mastered the starting off sequence, going back to the beginning again is all that is required. Watch that the traffic light has not gone back to red in the meantime. Especially REMEMBER, after a stall and before you re-start the engine, that physical check... that the handbrake is on and that you have returned to neutral correctly!

Clutch control starting off must become instinctive not just for the smooth take-off but for manoeuvring in any confined space; for example, on Test the three-point-turn and the reverse into a limited opening (Chapter 12), will be a shambles without it.

For these Test manoeuvres you have also got to be able to make the car move very slowly, over small distances. Try this out *now*. From the "both feet rock-steady" position (Steps 5/6, page 22) you release the handbrake as usual. Next, instead of full continuous smooth clutch release, you only release the pedal a tiny fraction, until the car just begins to move, barely perceptibly. The tiny amount you raise the pedal may be only a millimetre.

Hold the clutch in this new position, so that you keep the car moving at the speed of a snail for half a minute. In that time try to cover no more than three metres, neither going faster or actually stopping until the time is up. To prevent any stop on the way – or the opposite, running away too fast – you may need to alter the clutch pedal position up or down by a miniscule fraction here and there, but *never* like some yo-yo! You keep the accelerator where you have been holding it since Step 3, all the time; no more will be needed. When you can hit this snail's-speed target with ease whenever you want to, you have mastered slipping the clutch, a key element of *Car Driving In 2 Weeks*. Do not put up with an instructor who tries to rush you past this stage too quickly, solely in order to save wear on his clutch.

As well as learning to go as slowly as possible under clutch-slipping control, it is important for you to discover just how slowly you can move the car with the clutch fully up in 1st or 2nd gear (or, later on, in reverse), without stalling the engine. After a smooth take-off, instead of a gentle, firmer squeeze on the accelerator once the clutch is fully up as in Step 7, let your speed die down almost to a stall; then revive it with a featherlight touch back on the accelerator. With a little repetition and a few (inevitable) stalls thrown in, you will soon get the hang of just how slowly you can go with a gear fully engaged, clutch right up.

With only a little more practice after that, you will be able to "catch", and prevent, a stall of this kind in an even more controlled way. Instead of having to revive the engine by light re-acceleration (or having to stave off a stall by depressing the clutch below its connection point as you would for stopping), you will find that you can recapture a clutch-slipping position whilst still on the move. Just drop the clutch to the point it would be in Steps 5/6 of a smooth take-off. That gives the engine the chance to recover, and you can straightaway raise your revs to the point they would be for a smooth take-off. Without having stopped at any stage, you can now "take-off" again, simply by *smoothly* releasing the clutch pedal exactly as you would have, had you been carrying out Step 7 of a smooth take-off. Equally, if you wanted to move very slowly for a short distance before driving on again, you could. It would be just like doing the previous, snail-speed, exercise above, and then, instead of stopping, going on into the final clutch release of a smooth take-off.

Practice the technique. It will be extremely handy at junctions where, even though you may never quite have to stop, you need to go very, very slowly at some stage.

Starting On A Steep Hill

Steep uphill starts only terrify learners who haven't been properly taught. At no stage may the vehicle run backwards, *at all.* As soon as the smooth take-off on level ground is causing no problems, you should graduate to doing it on gentle slopes and after that find steep places for practice. The need to demonstrate a proper steep uphill start is certain to occur during your Test. If you have learned the right moment to release the handbrake for a level road start (Step 6, page 23), you will have no difficulty, however steep the hill. The only difference is that, when you set and hold the accelerator from Step 3, you need to maintain up to about twice the engine revs usually required, perhaps a little more if the hill is extremely steep. But there is no need to make the engine "scream". With the extra power on and the clutch being held at the "rarin' to go" point, there will be enough forward force to prevent any running back as you release the handbrake.

As on the level, there need be no rush to go when you release the handbrake. Hold the feet where they are, and the car will remain still 'til you are ready. (Normally, you would not wait deliberately, but the point is you could if you wanted.) Further smooth clutch release, and being ready smoothly to increase acceleration more if needed, and you are away!

1st gear is essential for an uphill start. It is also the usual choice for a level start, in order to be certain you will have sufficient power (e.g. especially at crossroads, etc.). For a *downhill* start, 2nd gear may be used. As there may be no need to accelerate, your procedure can leave out raising the engine revs. Simply release the handbrake (and footbrake if you have been holding it) at the "rarin' to go" moment, as you release the clutch. It will not matter if the brakes are off a fraction early on downhills, and knowing this helps you discover how to release the clutch and brakes in one flowing movement. Once the car is rolling, accelerate smoothly as required. Notice that on a dramatically steep downhill you may not want to accelerate;

indeed you may need the immediate benefit of "engine braking" as discussed in the next chapter and in Chapter 5.

3

STOPPING

The Order In Which To Learn

After the smooth take-off, I repeat that your first priority is to learn to stop. Normal stops, including pulling in to the kerb if you are going to park, come first, then emergency stops. In order to make progress with safe stopping, you will need to develop, at the same time, skill in steering and gear changing. The next two chapters deal with them. Take the time *you* need to grasp each technique really well at the beginning. Do not be rushed. Then excellence in basic car control will be yours, ready for the "deep end" of traffic in Part Two. You can enhance this early competence in car handling still further, and introduce reversing, if your instructor will also take you to suitable places to begin learning the manouevres you have to do on Test. See Chapter 12. To tuck these under your belt well before beginning much general driving experience, adds a great boost to confidence.

Normal Stops

The brake pedal is the centre one. When you press it, all wheels are braked. The mechanism is hydraulic and quite separate from the handbrake. That is mechanical and is only used for holding the car when stopped and for parking. The handbrake usually only works on one pair of wheels (most often the back pair) and, except in the event of footbrake failure, is never used for stopping.

You slow or stop the car, after noting from your mirrors whether it will be safe, by transferring your right foot on to the footbrake. Then, you gradually increase your pressure on the pedal according to how quickly you want to reduce speed. Do not stamp on it. This is a mistake, even in emergency. When you are *stopping*, you must also depress the clutch pedal to just below its connection point during the last car length before you pull up.

Putting the clutch pedal down disconnects the engine from the wheels and prevents stalling, *irrespective of the gear you are in.* Otherwise, with the engine still driving the car "against the brakes", it is bound to stall by the time you have stopped. As a guide, the engine warns it is about to cut out by a "cough", and the gear stick "quivers". Get the clutch pedal down just before this happens. Experience tells you when. It is safer and smooths the ride for passengers if you also slightly ease your brake pedal pressure during the last little distance. This enables you to let the car roll to a comfortable stop instead of with a final slight jerk.

Once stopped, set the handbrake, return the gear to neutral and release the footbrake and clutch pedals. Check behind in your mirrors in case you are now blocking someone's road. Be prepared to move on if it would then be easier for them to pass.

The Mirrors-Addict
Even in the quiet place where you will be making your first stops you must begin mirrors-addiction. It is so basic to driving, you will notice I'm getting you started before you even learn changing up and down the gears. *Every time* you slow down or stop (other than in emergency) you must first check your mirrors so that you can make suitable allowance to give those behind ample warning.

But there is more to becoming a mirrors-addict than merely checking them whenever you are about to move off, slow or stop, change lane, turn, overtake, or do any of the other things for which the Highway Code demands a mirrors check. A really skilled driver maintains a running mirrors' picture. Although such advanced drivers never take their eyes off the road in front for more than a split second for each mirrors-glance, they know what is happening behind, all the time, and they are acutely aware whenever anyone may be creeping up alongside, or passing.

The best drivers are thus *always prepared,* should an emergency arise when the position behind may be crucial in deciding instantly the right course of action. In emergency there may be no time to look again.

Although in law it is generally held to be that driver's fault if someone runs into the back of you when you are stopped, this is no excuse for stopping without sufficient warning. In these practice stops, remember that a driver following you, will see no traffic reason for a stop and therefore may not expect it. His or her only warning, in this circumstance, will be your brakelights, which come on as soon as you touch the pedal. He or she should, of course, be watching to see what your brakelights are going to mean, but a slow-down arm signal would give positive confirmation. The earlier you can learn to give one – at times when your reason for stopping may not be patently clear to others – the better. See Chapter 8.

Practice Stops

You must practise stopping, a great deal, before going on the open road; practise so much that doing it correctly becomes instinctive. Do straightforward gentle stops initially – making sure, as you begin to change up and down the gears, that you can stop just as happily whichever gear you happen to be in. It is only through practice that you can build up a mental picture of how to slow up evenly, with the car coming to a stop at exactly the place you intend.

When you have made some progress, you can try combining the stopping, with pulling in to the kerb-side to a neatly parked position. This is described at the end of this chapter. Always add a left flashing indicator signal for pull-ins, so others see what you are up to. See Chapter 8, page 75.

Just as important as signals to help drivers behind, is to learn to space out your stops so that those drivers have plenty of time to take heed.

Remember this "giving time" concept. Throughout your driving career you are going to meet moments when first reactions tend to make you brake too much, too hastily, instead of gauging the minimum degree of braking which – spread over the distance available – will slow or stop you comfortably and with some spare margin.

Other than in emergency, make it your habit always to brake gently to begin with – then progressively harder, only if necessary. Experience will teach you how to even out any further braking required for a particular traffic situation. This avoids ever slowing too sharply, or more than is needed.

This habitually gentle first touch on your brake should save you from those crackpots who so often get up your back bumper. It brings on your brakelights and gives them the extra time their mutton-heads need.

Mirrors-addiction boosts your chances of spotting such clever clots whilst they are zooming up to get on your tail. Once close, remember they can remain at large in your mirrors' blind spots (see fig. 31) for surprising lengths of time, especially those clots on two wheels. To be hidden for half a mile is not unusual.

The spare margin I talked of above is another aspect to giving time, in this case to yourself. Once your judgment confirms your brakes will stop you *well short* of where needed, you are in control for evening out the rest of the braking. You do not stop short in normal conditions but *making sure you could* gives you a double advantage; it confirms your brakes are O.K. and it gives early warning if a surface is skiddy. If anything is amiss it gives you room for a fighting chance to do something about it. Believe me, the day will come that you are very glad to have made this built-in safety margin an automatic part of the way you drive: your brakes could fail...your shoe could collapse on the pedal...

Emergency Stop Under Control (On Test)

As soon as you can stop normally, the emergency drill must be ingrained. On Test you will be asked to do an emergency stop unless a real emergency happens to have occurred. The examiner will say, "Some time soon, I will want you to demonstrate an emergency stop. I will say STOP and at the same time tap like this on the dashboard with my papers." However the instruction is given, it will be precise. Immediately you get the signal, STOP, as fast as you can. Do not worry about danger from behind; *stop*. (The examiner has checked behind.)

Should the signal to stop be given as you are about to change gear, ignore the gear change and stop. Some examiners give this emergency stop as you have just got round a turn. It does not matter. Wherever you are, *stop*.

Do not worry about the mirrors, or a slow-down arm signal, get your foot firmly on to the brake *fast, and follow immediately on the clutch pedal to prevent stalling*.

BOTH FEET DOWN.

Both hands must stay on the wheel to keep as straight as possible.

When the car is at a standstill, set the handbrake, bring the gear lever into neutral and release the foot pedals, but do not switch off the engine. You can expect the examiner to say, "drive on" almost straightaway, before anyone comes up behind.

The emergency stop, like everything else on Test, must be demonstrated to the examiner *under control.*

The anti-lock braking systems now widely available on new cars transform controllability in this and other respects. They will be examined later, from page 36. First we must discuss the problems of controlled braking still faced by the vast majority of drivers in cars without these systems.

Although your foot must flash to the brake pedal and press firmly, how much additional pressure you dare use, and how swiftly, is going to depend on how the tyres are gripping the road. To stamp hard on the brakes in "blind" panic can induce an immediate dangerous skid in which some or all of your wheels lock. A "locked" wheel is one that has stopped turning and is sliding instead.

When you come to your first live practice of emergency stops, open your window. Then you can hear immediately a wheel locks. It will screech on dry tarmac or slither on wet road. You will soon learn to recognise what it feels like, even with the window shut again. The instant it happens, you scotch it by *easing* off the footbrake to let the wheels roll. The sliding stops instantaneously, allowing you to *resume full braking* just as fast as your brain can flash the message to your feet. If the car slides again, you repeat easing off and then rapidly back on, perhaps several times, all the way down to a standstill. The object is to gain the maximum possible braking for the least amount of wheel(s) locking.

The reason you *must* keep the steering as straight as you can is that the front wheels are otherwise more likely to lock and skid. If they lock, steering control is lost 'til they come free. This makes emergency stopping on a bend, with the cornering attitude of the car tending to throw you off course as well, very dicey. Part of the solution might be to straighten those wheels at once, for as long as you dared whilst you were trying to brake. However, I return to the problems of skidding in Chapter 19; for Test emergency stop practice, stick to straight road!

The ability to spot the onset of a wheel-locking skid and deal with it within a trice is essential to the emergency stop *under control.* Then the repeat, **on/ease-off/on** braking, provides the skilled driver's key to the fastest and safest stop, particularly when the surface is slippery.

This is because, technically, the best braking is obtained by nearly, *but not quite,* locking the wheels, from the time you first put on the brakes 'til the moment you stop. Success achieving that ideal best braking, essentially has to be discovered by negative feedback. You come closest to the ideal by making (small) mistakes. By braking too hard you induce a skid; recognising the error, instantly flashes the ease-off signal from your brain. Your mental picture, built up from previous mistakes, also warns when you are on the verge of wheel-lock. These feedbacks combine without conscious thought once you have some experience of emergency stopping. The skilled use of them, which you must acquire, only comes with much practice. That practice will also help you appreciate how, as a rule, the nearer you are to a stop the more you are able to increase braking pressure without locking a wheel.

The Need For Practice
You need lots of emergency stop practice right up to your Test. It is worthwhile pre-sharpening your feet emergency reactions by practising whilst stationary. This saves wear on brake linings and tyres, as you learn to transmit from brain to feet like lightning. Once you achieve life-saving quickness you will be much safer. Indeed one purpose of the Test emergency stop is to convince the examiner you can react fast, as well as correctly.

With your feet reactions tuned, move to live practice on straight, level *dry* road. Leave wet, skiddy surfaces, 'til later, when you can already stop fast and safely on the dry. Make sure nothing is following and that the road is clear and safe. Start from speeds *below* 20 m.p.h. (miles per hour) in 1st or 2nd gear. Remember that you have got to learn emergency stopping *under* maximum *control*. Build your experience of such stopping from higher speeds, gradually, until you feel confident emergency stopping on the dry from up to 40 or 45 m.p.h. in the higher gears. (Note: For emergency stops from above 30 m.p.h. see also the lower half of the page overleaf.)

Then, when you move on to wet weather practice, begin very cautiously, once again on straight, level road from *below* 20 m.p.h. You will find the difference between wet and dry is spectacular because wheels lock so much more easily. Build your wet conditions knowledge bit by bit just as you did on the dry.

After level road emergency stop practice, try uphill then downhill. This will implant in your mind how *very, very much harder* it is to stop downhill because of the car's momentum. Conversely, it will reveal that stopping uphill seems just a little easier.

Real Emergencies

I included the word *safest* above in describing **on/ease-off/on** braking. I explained that, when front wheels lock, steering control is lost, and stressed your having the steering straight to reduce the possibility. However, sometimes in a real emergency you may be forced to swerve as well as brake and you need the wheels rolling to give you the chance.

What makes the braking method I give widely accepted as safest is not just the technical factor described. It also instils an "instinctive" understanding of what to do to keep the wheels rolling and therefore steerable. And this makes lifting off the brake, if you have to whilst you swerve, an almost instantaneous reflex action.

Suppose a young child has dashed across in front of you, tripped and fallen, and that, even as you desperately try to stop, swerving round has to take precedence. *You* must be alive to your available options that may save that child's life. It is no good skidding helplessly towards hitting the tiny tot, hypnotised as the rabbit by the weasel. Act to swing clear.

Research On Learning The Emergency Stop Routine

The **BOTH FEET DOWN** method of emergency stopping I have outlined is the best way to learn, at the beginning. It prevents you ever stalling the engine, which can cause a panic. Therefore master the **BOTH FEET DOWN** method until you are doing it without thought and you feel safe with it. However, research by tyre companies and others, has shown that fractionally more efficient stopping should result if the brake is applied alone, and the clutch not depressed until the car has almost stopped. This is because the small "braking effect" of the engine (not being accelerated!) is additional to the effect of the brakes. (Engine braking is explained on page 44.) You will find it easy to adopt this later application of the clutch as experience grows with practice. In practical terms there isn't time to hold off the clutch when you are *emergency* stopping from under about 30 m.p.h. anyway, but do aim to use the latter way for emergency stops from any speed above that, by the time of your Test.

After learning the later clutch method and with a good many miles behind you, but preferably before your Test, an emergency stop or two from 60-70 m.p.h. can be tried. Choose a quiet time and a wide, clear, dry, dual carriageway. Your instructor should demonstrate this stop first, and both of you discuss what has happened, before you try on the same piece of road. Choose a conspicuous roadside mark from which to begin stopping each time, so that you can look back afterwards and see how far it really was. The greatest care must be exercised because you are to learn for the first time how very much harder it is to stop from, for example, 70 m.p.h., than from 40 m.p.h., and how much more distance is required. It is likely to be a shock that will serve you well in all your driving career – as a grim reminder to maintain a safe following distance behind other cars at high speeds.

You do not double the distance as you double the speed, as some drivers seem to think. Look in the Highway Code and you will find average figures for dry roads. Well over double the distance is needed from 70 m.p.h., compared with 40 m.p.h., but 70 m.p.h. is less than twice as fast as 40 m.p.h.! But figures are hard to translate into what it feels and looks like when you are forced to stop from 70 m.p.h. This is why I recommend these early practice emergency stops, which help you visualise the dangers.

Increased distance is only one extra hazard of emergency stopping from high speed. *From higher speeds,* even on a dry road, it is not uncommon for the attempt to stop in a straight line to finish up spinning round, out of control 180° or more!

Why? Because of the high speed, the front wheels – even with most of the car's weight thrown forward on to them – cannot normally lock initially; it's physically impossible unless the surface is exceptionally skiddy. But *the back wheels* – with the weight of the car lifted *off* them – are, by the same token, prone to locking earlier than might be expected. (In fact some 4/5ths of actual braking occurs at the front wheels.) Once those back wheels start to lock, the back of the car may skid out to whichever side the combination of weight and other factors takes it.

There is, then, a tendency it's important to be aware of when braking from *very* high speeds – a "pre-disposition" for the back wheels to lock and slide *first,* potentially setting the car off into a spin.

If the back does slide substantially off course before you react (which you do by instantly slackening your brake pressure momentarily, and by steering temporarily towards the side the back has gone), you can be into a spin very quickly. So don't "freeze" at the wheel or on the brakes. However, recovery is normally swift, and there should be no cause for this situation to get out of hand – provided you are aware of the danger, and awake!

Before we look at anti-lock brakes and then return to ordinary stopping, I ask you to remember that almost every emergency – every accident – is unexpected. You could face one on your first live lesson. That is why basic emergency reactions must be taught first.

Anti-Lock Brakes

Although the various systems now fitted to different makes of car offer differing degrees of sophisticated excellence, they all take over from the driver the need to worry about wheels locking, or any (consequent) loss of steering control. However hard you press the brake pedal, the system reduces the brake pressure, at each individual wheel according to its need, sufficiently so that no wheel ever locks. Whenever you put your foot hard on the brake in emergency, the car simply stops in the minimum possible distance.

None of the **on/ease-off/on** braking, gone into above in such detail for the ordinary car, applies. Indeed, if you change to an anti-lock braked car after being used to one with an ordinary system, you have to remember in emergency braking, NOT to be prepared for the easing-off/and back on again, and to be ready instead, simply to keep the footbrake on hard.

You also have to build another life-saving fact into your thinking when you drive with anti-lock brakes. Because the front wheels cannot lock or slide, *you can still steer,* even when braking for your own or someone else's life. Whereas in the past few pages I have stressed how locked-brake front wheel skidding means steering control disappears, and how you must keep the steering straight as much as possible to help prevent it, with these new brakes you no longer need to think so much in those terms.

In the example I gave under **Real Emergencies,** page 34, you would be able to brake *and* steer round the child, all at once, and with a much better chance of saving that kidling.

It would be wrong to suggest violent swerving during emergency braking, other than in dire necessity, because that could mean losing control too, but this ability to steer does provide a massively powerful new level of life-saving control. The combination of this steerability and the non-skid anti-lock feature, makes these systems so different, that any experienced drivers who drive with them for the first time should take care to familiarise themselves with the new options at their feet and fingertips. A few trial emergency stops ought to impress their subconscious reflexes with the altered responses which are required with these brakes in comparison to the ordinary-braked vehicles they have been used to.

Stopping Whenever The Traffic Situation Demands

You frequently have to make a smooth stop for red traffic lights, zebra crossings, or whenever the stream of traffic you are in stops for any reason.

It is a bad driver who is forced into situations where he or she has to stop violently. You could fail the Test for it. Do not rush up behind stopped traffic, or towards traffic lights, or on the approach to a pedestrian crossing. Arrive gently, ready to stop smoothly. The advanced driver will almost never make an emergency stop. If you have to make them repeatedly you are displaying inexperience.

At each such stop of more than a few seconds' duration, your basic rule must be to apply the handbrake and put the gear into neutral. Then release the footbrake and the clutch. When ready to move on, use the full **Smooth Take-Off** routine.

Sometimes, however, when the stop is brief and you are able to move on almost straightaway, you can instead, after applying the handbrake, select 1st gear immediately, directly from whatever gear you were in, keeping the clutch down. This jumps you straight to the beginning of Step 3 of the smooth take-off. However, you must never sit waiting in gear like this for more than a few seconds. This would cause undue wear to the clutch mechanism.

For a *very* short stop *on an absolutely level road*, it is acceptable to hold the car on the footbrake and avoid having to use the handbrake at all, provided it is done skilfully. (But you must never sit with neither brake holding you!) To move ahead, you simply adapt your smooth take-off routine to keeping that footbrake holding the car until you are you also holding the clutch steady as at the beginning of Step 5. From there you niftily switch your right foot so as to boost the accelerator, and then hold it, ready to carry out as you would normally the appropriate parts of Steps 6 and 7.

Doing without the handbrake is inappropriate when you are the front driver to stop at a junction. You must use the handbrake then, both for safety, and to satisfy the examiner – even if the stop is only for a second or two.

Whilst on the subject of traffic stops, it's worth mentioning that one of the commonest accidents is a rear-end "shunt". If you are unlucky enough to be hit from behind, then by having the handbrake or footbrake on, the car should not be booted forward quite so violently, and you may at least partially save yourself awful whip-lash neck injuries, not to mention possibly being shot into the car in front!

There is a cute habit which may save you from being the victim of a shunt. It is valuable when you become back marker of a queue, especially one where faster moving traffic from a long way behind may not see in time that you are stopping. The idea is to leave yourself an extra car length or so, in hand, when you pull up. Once you see in your mirrors that the next two or three drivers to arrive are in control for stopping, you can close up the space. But if any are about to stove into the queue, the space you have left for moving up into can save the day...if you are watching your mirrors.

Pulling In To Stop Next To The Nearside (Or Left Hand) Kerb

Remember to use your left flashing indicator whenever pulling in like this. You might want to add a left turn arm signal too. See Chapter 8, page 77. Learners often find it difficult, both forwards and in reverse, to judge the distance from the kerb for such a stop at the edge. Practice is vital to learn how to place the vehicle close in. You must first gain a "feel" for whether the car is properly parallel to the kerb, and second, for just how far away from it you are. A piece of string in your drive-way, or the lines in an empty car park, are a great help before trying beside an actual kerb. You thus avoid damage, which may later cause a lethal "blow out" at high speed, to your tyres or wheelrims. (See page 179.) And you can practise for "right hand" kerbs too. As mentioned before, early practice of the Test manoeuvres which you will find in Chapter 12, will be a great help to you in judging how big the car is, exactly how far out from the kerb it is, and so on.

When you pull in, the car should finish parked parallel to the kerb, and with the nearest side tyres under 1-2 of their own widths out from the edge. The lazy driver who leaves the front or the back of the car sticking out, or the entire car a door width out, is an inconsiderate, dangerous pest. You can accept under 1-2 tyre widths to begin with; for really good driving (and should you have to park in a very narrow street), make your objective to be under 1 tyre width.

4

STEERING

BEWARE! LOOK WHERE YOU ARE GOING. Your brain, absorbed by the details of *how to steer,* becomes deadly dangerous if it ever draws your attention off the road as a result – even for a split second! Never take *both* hands off the steering wheel at once. If one hand is needed briefly for a gear change or a signal, the other *must* be on the wheel. At all other times, KEEP BOTH HANDS ON THE WHEEL. Never mind just satisfying the examiner; other lives depend on you, and your guardian angel sees all!

Holding The Wheel
Other than for turning, hold the wheel between the "ten to two" and "quarter to three" clock-face positions, as in fig. 3.

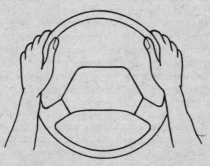

Fig. 3. Steering wheel hold suggested when going straight.

There is no need to grip the wheel like grim death all the time. That is tiring and leads to a jerky meandering style. All that is required for driving along a straight road is a firm but light hold to keep the car rock-steady. On bumpy roads, or ones which slope unusually much towards the edge, you may need a slight correction from time to time for arrow straightness but there is no need to "steer" consciously. Doing that constantly, makes the car wander, funny as that may seem.

A gentle bend or curve will need very little steering movement; your hands may not need to alter their basic position at all. However, for more than the mildest sweep to the right or left – anything remotely describable as a corner – you must adopt the method for turning I now give below.

Steering For Turns

To turn right you turn the steering wheel clockwise. (As turning left merely needs the instructions applied anti-clockwise, I will not go on to bore you with the intimate details for that!)

With the right hand holding it firmly, pull the wheel from ten past the hour, down to 25 minutes past. During this downward pull, the left hand grip is relaxed, and this hand, still round the wheel at all times, is dropped to the 20 minutes to the hour position. It arrives at the same moment that the right hand reaches 25 past. Now, with a firmly held upward "push" of the left hand and a relaxed, sliding, right hand, the wheel turning is continued. The hands reach the five minutes to and ten past positions near the top, at the same moment (just as they arrived at the end of the downward movement simultaneously), ready for more repeat movements as required. As soon as you are round the corner, the wheel has to be turned the opposite way by similar movements – and quite vigorously for tight turns – for the purpose of straightening up and completing the turn.

In most cars there is a degree of self-centering built into the steering mechanism, so that the steering wheel would return to straight if you just let it go. It is wrong and dangerous to let go completely (as the car is then out of control). But for *very small amounts* of steering it is acceptable driving to allow the steering wheel to return to the straight-on position itself. Relax the grip of both hands, whilst the wheel slides back through your fingers loosely held around the rim in the proper positions between "ten to two" and a "quarter to three".

You must never cross your hands or arms on the steering wheel. This is not likely to happen when you are driving along but it can become a temptation at corners, or when you are reversing or manoeuvring. Never succumb to it.

"Wandering"

Wandering is common whenever the beginner has to have one hand off the wheel for changing gear, or for giving an arm signal.

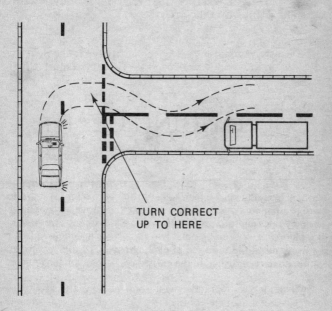

TURN CORRECT
UP TO HERE

Fig. 4.   Failing to straighten up quickly enough after a right turn.

A little specific practice at single-hand steering in the early lessons on quiet roads, whilst you polish up gear changing and learn to give a slow-down arm signal, quickly eradicates the problem.

However, wandering is also common even among so-called experienced drivers, those who mistakenly try to change gear at the same time that they are turning at a junction. Never change gear whilst turning. Change down for greater control, *before* you turn. Then steer round with both hands on the wheel. Once you are round, be sure that you have the vehicle under control and driving straight, before you change up again.

Another typical beginner's error is if, in completing a turn, he or she fails to straighten up the steering wheel at the right moment and/or quickly enough; the car goes too far round the corner, and, as a result, swings dangerously out towards oncoming traffic, as in fig. 4.

5

CHANGING GEAR

If you are learning with automatic gears see Chapter 13, but read this one too.

You have to be able to change gear practically from the moment you can start, steer and stop safely. You must learn to change up and down the gearbox on the move as required, scarcely needing to pause for thought, and without *ever* having to look down. Your hand must leave the steering wheel only for the minimum time required at each change. All this technique should be accomplished in the early days before you leave quiet roads.

By listening and practice you soon acquire the ability to interpret the "language" of the engine, and change gear when it "tells" you – relating your knowledge to whether the road is flat, uphill or down, and to your speed. To start with, however, you need a foolproof formula by which to change gear at the correct time.

Here is that formula. It relates to a four forward speed gearbox because, even with five gears, you use the first four in the same way. I describe 4th gear as **Top**, partly because that is how it was always known before 5th gears became common, and partly because a 5th gear is rarely more powerful, as explained towards the end of this chapter.

Except where traffic conditions or speed limits mean you need to hold back, you should move up the gears swiftly, making use of their best range to pick up speed smartly. There are few

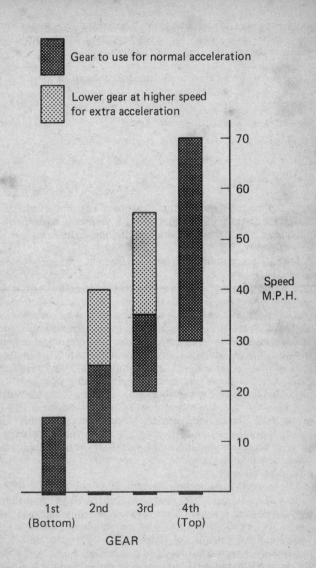

Fig. 5. Gear changes in relation to speed.

more annoying drivers than those who invariably dawdle when they could get going. However, unless you require rapid acceleration, never "flog" the engine in any gear.

Formula For Normal Acceleration

RANGE	MAXIMUM	GEAR
Up to 10 or 15 m.p.h.		1st (**Bottom**)
10-25 m.p.h.	(or a rough max. of 40 m.p.h.)	2nd
20-35 m.p.h.	(or a rough max. of 55 m.p.h.)	3rd
30-35 m.p.h. and over		4th (**Top**)

The formula is for normal acceleration of an average car. Fig. 5 shows the formula diagrammatically. If you want *extra* acceleration from a slow speed, as when overtaking, go up to *maximum* figures shown.

Initially you will find you have to glance at your speedometer to see when to change gear, but very soon association of ideas makes the "language" of the engine sub-consciously understood and the formula redundant.

As the formula and fig. 5 both indicate, it is not essential to change at exact speeds. When climbing a hill the normal speeds in a gear might be increased by 5 m.p.h., or when going downhill, reduced by 2 or 3 m.p.h. Then, should it be tending to run away too fast, the "braking effect" of the engine will help to slow the car's progress down the hill. (Engine braking occurs when, instead of the engine under acceleration driving the road wheels and thus the car, the momentum of the car begins to try to reverse the process and actually accelerate the engine. The resistance of the engine to running faster than you would expect for your accelerator setting in the particular gear you are in, can easily be felt holding the car back, especially if your foot is right off the accelerator.)

The normal *acceleration* formula does not mean that you cannot drive along in 2nd, 3rd or Top gear at lower speeds than those indicated; you can. Most cars are perfectly happy in Top gear down to about 20 m.p.h., wherever conditions are such that you cannot go more quickly. Indeed, you would never trail along indefinitely in slow traffic at 25 m.p.h. in 2nd or 3rd; you would get up into (or stay in) Top (4th) gear, only dropping to 3rd or 2nd when the need arose to accelerate, or you needed extra power to go uphill, or you wanted "engine braking" control because the road started to go downhill.

How To Hold The Gear Lever

There is no need to clasp the gear lever knob tightly, except when the reverse gear is such that the lever has, for example, to be *lifted* into position.

Allow your palm to "mould" itself around the knob and then lead the gear lever in the direction wanted, with your palm facing the way you want it to go, and pushing or pulling gently.

Visualise a capital letter H under the floor of your car, with the various lines which form the H, as "lanes" or "channels". Each selected gear of the four main forward gears is at the *end* of a "lane" to one corner of the H. The crossbar of the H is the neutral "channel". Reverse is normally outside the H, as would be a 5th gear if the car has one, these positions being taken off an extension to the H crossbar. When the lever is in the neutral lane, the gears are disconnected. Look at fig. 1 for typical gear positions.

Whenever you change, use a confident, easy through movement. Where the change involves sideways movement across the neutral channel, allow a slight pause as the lever self-seeks (or you direct it) over, ready to slip into the next gear.

The Clutch When Changing Gear

While gears are changed the engine must be disengaged by using the clutch. Use of the clutch for the smooth take-off is quite different and has been explained already.

The procedure for changing gear on the move is:

1. Depress clutch pedal (below the connection point is enough), simultaneously releasing the accelerator.

2. Move gear lever through neutral to next gear required. Return your hand to the steering wheel.

3. Immediately you have selected the new gear, allow the clutch pedal to come up fully, smoothly, in one unbroken movement.

4. As your left foot is completing **3** your right foot should be smoothly re-engaging the accelerator.

The degree you take up acceleration again depends on the reason for the gear change. It may be hardly at all if you are changing down to slow down, quite a lot if the downward change was to retain speed uphill, or moderate if you are merely changing up to Top having reached cruising speed. To avoid any jerk, your take-up on the accelerator must always be progressive, never sharp.

Where To Change Gear

Imagine that you are driving along a straight, busy road, in Top, and in a stream of traffic travelling steadily at 40 m.p.h. Suppose you are the eighth vehicle in the stream. For some reason unknown to you the traffic is losing speed. Because of this you must slow down. You have an eye on your mirrors – see page 29. You raise your foot off the accelerator pedal to lose speed, and the speedometer reading falls.

As speed drops to around 25 m.p.h. you slip into 3rd gear.

You will still be travelling with the traffic, but at 25 m.p.h. instead of 40 m.p.h. In 3rd, you are prepared for picking up speed smartly to keep up if the stream soon moves faster again, but suppose the traffic now moves still slower, and shows no sign of picking up speed; if your speedometer now falls to as low as 15 m.p.h. you drop into 2nd gear.

After a short spell hovering around 10-15 m.p.h., you may notice that the traffic is now moving more quickly again. You gently accelerate to match the new speed. Your speed is rapidly restored to around 20 m.p.h., and therefore you change up to 3rd gear. The stream continues to build up speed, so, as before, you go on gently increasing your squeeze on the accelerator. It is not long before your speedometer again touches 30 m.p.h. You can now slip back into top, and, assuming the stream then goes on to get itself back to a steady 40 m.p.h., accelerate a little, or as required, to enable you to keep in your position.

So it continues, with gear changes up and down as occasion demands.

For an uphill stretch we have already touched on the fact that it may be necessary for extra pulling power, to change down from 4th to 3rd gear, or even to 2nd, depending on the gradient. Change down early so that you can maintain as much of your speed as possible, and briskly. Otherwise you will slow down people behind unnecessarily and much to their irritation.

We also noted how, if you are a wise driver, you take advantage of engine braking for greater car control going down steep hills. This is better driving and saves brake linings. You slow to a speed appropriate for 3rd gear and change down to it before starting the descent. You can, if necessary, then brake on the way down as well, but you are mainly making use of "engine braking".

For an unusually steep hill, say 1 in 6 (17%), or steeper, slow right down and get into 2nd gear before the start, because it can be difficult to make an extra change (3rd to 2nd) during the descent.

Should 2nd gear subsequently prove to be unnecessarily low for the hill, it is simple to change back up to 3rd again, unlike the other way round.

The difficult change, however, is not impossible, and it is worth practice at a suitably steep downhill. Speed must be brought down with the footbrake to well within 2nd gear limits first, before the change down into it can be made; afterwards, if speed still begins to "run away" despite the extra engine resistance, the footbrake will have to be used again.

Readers may have heard the terms "gas in the gears" and/or "double-de-clutch". The full double-de-clutch is more complex but is only necessary with a vintage or older car. However, the learner can master gassing in the gears. It is a half-way house, both for more polished car control in everyday driving and, as explained below, for safety in the event of having to change down at any higher speed than normal.

The procedure is only used for changing down. The objective is, whilst you have your clutch pedal down, to pre-match the relative speeds of the engine and the driving wheels on the road, in the new ratio which will be provided by the lower gear. (At the same road speed the engine has to work much faster in a low gear than in a high gear.)

During Stage (2) of the gear change (see page 45), you blip the accelerator to provide extra engine revs which will then be just beginning to die away at (3), as your clutch pedal release completes. These remaining higher revs as the gear becomes engaged to take up of the drive, should prevent any jerk being felt by passengers, or any chance of ill-matched reconnection of the wheels to the engine causing "wheel-snatch", or perhaps setting off a skid. A stronger rev tends to be needed for a change from 3rd to 2nd gear than is usually required from 4th to 3rd. The higher up the speed range for the lower gear you are going down into, the more revs you need.

Learners often wonder what the limits are for a change down to 3rd gear from 4th, if you have left it rather late going downhill and the vehicle is gathering speed. Although it is *not* advised for normal circumstances, you can go from 4th to 3rd in most cars at up to 55-60 m.p.h. On a high performance car the figure could be a little higher. However, the clutch pedal must be released exceptionally *smoothly* after the change. In addition, you must have "gassed in" the gear as explained above. Otherwise, a sudden jerk of your foot off the clutch pedal, or not having high enough pre-matching revs, can produce a frightening wheel-snatch-induced skid, especially on a wet surface.

A late change from 3rd to 2nd is equally possible if properly handled, but speed then must be below 40-45 m.p.h.

1st gear (Bottom) is really only used for starting off from rest. You would *not* include it in the general run of gear changing that I have described for keeping pace as you go along. Firstly, the number of occasions you might need to harness the extra pulling power of 1st gear from on the move is very small. Secondly, except on cars which have effective synchromesh on this Bottom gear to help it slip in easily, trying to get down into 1st from 2nd tends to cause a loud graunch, unless speed is down almost to a standstill.

Nevertheless, you have to be able to make this change successfully, because there are times when you do need to drop down into 1st gear on the move: you might find it necessary in a stop-start uphill queue; safety may demand it.

An example of the safety aspect could be when joining a major road out of a fantastically steep uphill side road. Because of checking that the major road will be clear, your approach speed to the junction will be down to hardly moving anyway. If experience then warns you that the engine cannot pull the car up the final gradient in 2nd gear at any slower speed (or perhaps the engine is already faltering), you have two alternatives. You can choose to stop at the junction, regardless of whether or not the presence of traffic on the major road impels you to do so. Then you can start off in 1st gear when the way is clear, knowing that you can avoid any danger of stalling as the engine hauls the car up out on to the major road. Your other choice, which is better driving because it often saves a stop for people behind you as well, is to take 1st as soon as your speed falls below 10-15 m.p.h. Provided the major road remains clear, this then removes the need to stop when you reach the junction itself.

What is dangerous and you must NEVER do, is to attempt to go on in 2nd, and then find the engine stalls as you are half-way out...with perhaps, by then, major road traffic bearing down upon you.

Comfortably under 10 m.p.h., you should find the gear slips handily into 1st without any crunch, whatever the state of the car's synchromesh. However, it needs practice to be able to do this gear change quickly and keep the car moving, otherwise you can find that before you have completed it, the car has stopped and is already running back down the hill! You will be wise to perfect the technique early on. Gas the gear in for an even smoother change.

Should you decide to change gear for any reason, do it. Avoid repeatedly taking hold of the gear lever as if you are going to change, and then moving your hand back to the steering wheel. This indicates indecision. Test examiners observe it, and they may fail a learner who dithers continuously.

Gear Changing When You Approach A Traffic Hazard

You may be front marker approaching a traffic light which has only just changed to red, a zebra crossing where an "Indian file" of children has just started to cross, or a "Stop" sign. You are certain that you will have to stop. Change into 3rd gear as you get down to about 25 m.p.h.; draw gently to a halt. There is no need to go further down the gearbox when stopping is compulsory. When stopped, pull on the handbrake, come out of gear and take your feet off the footbrake and clutch – the examiner will be watching for safe procedure to hold the car steady while you wait.

If you are a dozen or so places behind the first car having to stop, you may get involved in several "mini" stops before you reach the basic reason for all the stopping. Unless it is a "stop" sign junction line (at which, by law, each of you has to stop in turn) you may not even need to stop by the time you get there. For these "mini" stops, if it is a level road and each one is just for a second, the alternative short-cut drill on page 37 may be appropriate, using 1st gear. But, where it is still necessary for you to stop when you reach the front, you must then use the full smooth take-off procedure.

Suppose that, instead of a certain stop, you are now approaching a traffic hazard where you *may* have to stop, such as give-way lines, or perhaps a pelican crossing when you are not sure whether a pedestrian standing nearby has pressed the button – in which case you may be the first to have to stop once the steady amber light comes on. In these sorts of circumstances, as you slow down and prepare to stop, you also change down into second when your speed falls below 15-20 m.p.h., so that you are cautiously ready to re-accelerate should the road turn out to be clear. You are no less ready for stopping but you should try not to stop unnecessarily. This can cause accidents. Drivers behind you will be annoyed if you hold them up without reason.

It is acceptable in circumstances such as those above, though in my view somewhat lazy, to omit 3rd gear, and stay in Top (4th), 'til speed is down ready to go direct to 2nd. In the same way there are a few occasions going up the gearbox to by-pass a gear if you do not need much acceleration, but be careful only to skip gears when it makes sense, guided by your instructor.

Coasting

Coasting means going along under momentum, either out of gear, or whilst holding the clutch down for unnecessarily long. Whatever speed you may be doing, it is banned because the car is then not fully *under control*. It follows that, when you are moving up to keep your place in a stop-start queue, you should release the clutch pedal fully for as much of the distance you are moving forward as is possible; you should avoid slipping the clutch unnecessarily (as even that might be classed by some as "coasting", and it would, in any case, cause excessive wear), and you should always wait 'til you are almost up to the point where you want to stop, before your clutch (and footbrake!) go down again.

If the pace has dropped under walking speed but you never quite have to stop, the purist rightly expects to see you go down to 1st gear on the move rather than holding on, slipping the clutch in 2nd. In practice, however, you will find 2nd has adequate power unless the road you are on is uphill. There, you will have to be able to take 1st on the move. To remind you how to do it, see page 48. If things reach the stage where you would have to slip the clutch in 1st, stop. Wait for those ahead to move on a few metres. See also page 26.

5th Gear

5th gears, although they can be used as low as 25-30 m.p.h., are really intended for cruising above 40-45 m.p.h. They help conserve petrol by allowing the engine to turn over more slowly; they also reduce noise and extend engine life. 5th gear need rarely be reached by a learner in town driving. In contrast, you naturally use it on the open road where you can, because of the advantages listed above. Surprisingly, the car's maximum speed in 4th (Top) may be little short of that possible in 5th. However, the rate of acceleration available will be better in 4th than in 5th, as will performance uphill. 4th is therefore usually a safer gear to be in for fast overtaking.

PART TWO
DRIVING THE CAR

6

DRIVING ALONG

Read Part Two here and study all of the Highway Code *before* you begin. It would be reckless to start driving before you can recognise all the important road signs, signals and markings. Test yourself with friends. The additional H.M.S.O. booklet, "Know Your Traffic Signs" is indispensable. Get one!

As you progress beyond the very quietest roads, extend your experience at a sensible rate. It is unsafe to hurl yourself into the rush hour on day one! Doing so is also very selfish; until you can keep up with traffic, you are only going to create unnecessary queues behind you.

Look Out!
Above all, *look where you are going*. Search ahead constantly, both near *and far,* watching for potential danger ahead and at either side. There is scarcely a moment in driving when the changing scene in front does not call for anticipation or reaction by you, to what is there. The examiner will notice what you miss...He or she is looking for first class anticipation, and awareness of what anyone else on foot or on wheels is going to do next.

You must prove your skill by acting upon what you see, adjusting speed, position or whatever, always in good time. This skill must include knowing what is behind you, not just when you are about to overtake or change lane, slow, turn, or stop – when a *confirming* check in the mirrors has to be *routine* – but by oft-repeated glances in the mirrors that keep you in touch.

The only exception to keeping your eyes all around the road is when you check your speedometer or warning instruments. Choose safe moments; they need but a tiny fraction of your attention.

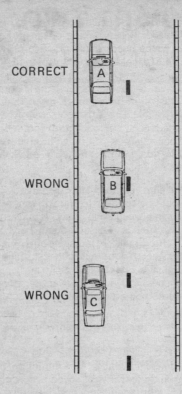

Fig. 6.   **A.** Correct travelling position on a road with only
one lane each way.

B. WRONG: risks colliding with oncoming traffic.

C. WRONG: risks accidents, or damage to
tyres – respectively from being too close to
the edge at junctions and from bumping the
kerb; also increases chances of picking up
punctures from debris in gutter.

The Ideal Travelling Position

The rule of the road in the U.K. is **you drive on the left.** Moving
off from the nearside kerb, there is no need to pull out fully at

once unless the road is obstructed. Keep well to the left until you have gathered speed. When pulling out from behind another parked vehicle (which needs much practice...), allow yourself plenty of extra time for snail's-pace control until you are clear of that vehicle. The examiner will ensure that this comes up on your Test. Take extra account of any traffic coming the other way. As you must pull out so much more than normal, and initially at a sharp angle across the road, your front offside wing can place them in danger, not to mention yourself! Besides that, the Highway Code rule that you *must* "**...give way to vehicles coming towards you before you pass parked vehicles...**", counts the same here as anywhere else.

Provided overall width allows for it well inside your own half of the road, it is best to drive around half-a-metre away from the nearside kerb. On very wide roads it could be a little more. See fig. 6. This should be no problem on wide urban roads and the big roads out of town, but be careful not to "hog" that part of your lane nearest the middle of the road, like "B" in fig. 6. Doing that, can make it supremely difficult, or impossible, for anyone to see past you in order to overtake safely. On country routes or narrow town streets you often have to stay closer in, with speeds reduced accordingly. Only maniacs speed on in narrow places, or "charge" through small gaps in the face of oncoming traffic. See my "final word" at the back of the book, warning about speed.

Whenever you go past a parked vehicle, or a line of them, you must leave sufficient clearance – a minimum of one door's opening width – and control your speed accordingly; someone may fling open a door; a hidden pedestrian could step out. See Chapter 17, "commandments" 8 and 9, now! This discipline must become fused into your driving nature.

On the bigger roads you must watch out for white lane arrows on the road. These are common at the approach to traffic lights, roundabouts, and some other junctions. (See fig. 7.) Their purpose is to speed the traffic-flow, but it does not work if motorists ignore them despite the fact that they are obligatory. Approaching any junction where there are lane arrows, look for the one which shows which lane to take for the direction you are going.

This is particularly important in heavy traffic. If you make a mistake you may find, for example, that you are then in the wrong lane, holding up the traffic-flow at a green filter arrow on a traffic light. You must not remain there causing an obstruction

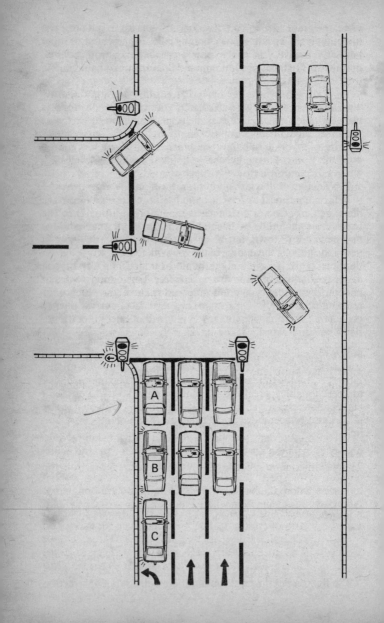

when the green arrow light, lights up. You must move on in the direction it shows if it applies to your lane. Re-adjust your route later. Otherwise you can expect angry hooting from behind, despite the Highway Code command that the horn should not be used as a rebuke.

Lane divisions on your own side of the road may also be marked on stretches between junctions, wherever the road is wide enough. Dual carriageway sections, if any, are sure to be so marked. Queuing or slow moving heavy traffic often spontaneously divides into lanes even where none are set out for the less busy times. The good drivers "think in lanes", helping each other and the traffic-flow. (Hordes of dodderers – of all ages – still do not!)

Which lane to choose when, and how to change lanes are discussed elsewhere. For the moment, take notice that the examiner watches to see that you normally keep to the middle of marked lanes when there are several on your side, and that you never straddle a lane line without good reason. Causing an unnecessary blockage for the next door lane can be marked against you, whether you are moving or stopped. So can chopping from one lane to another merely for temporary advantage.

Speed
You must keep within speed limits. You must also let your instructor guide you at all times, so that you never exceed a speed matched to your capabilities or to the road conditions. However, by the time of your Test, you are expected to be able to keep up with typical (law abiding) traffic, so that you don't create unnecessary queues behind you. On Test, all you need be is an average-speed driver. Let the speed-merchants pass you by.

Bends In The Road
The safe maximum speed for a bend and how to take it, from the

Fig. 7. A left filter green arrow has come on for the left lane of traffic at the bottom of this picture. Red still holds the other two straight-on lanes. Driver **A** is in the **WRONG** lane for going straight ahead, and *must now turn left* to avoid holding up **B** and **C**.

point of view of stability and skid avoidance, is dealt with fully in Chapter 19. As an "L", your instructor should keep you well under that safe maximum.

At a blind bend you must also be slow enough to stop half-way round the corner, if you have to. See page 61. Amongst the myriad of possibilities for danger, suppose you come across a walker or a cyclist, etc., on your own side, and no room to pass because of a lorry coming the other way. Or, that that lorry suddenly appears on your side because it's trying to pass a small roadworks or something similar. In either event, unless you have controlled your speed so as to be able to stop in an instant, you are in grave trouble.

Positioning on approach to a left hander, keep well into your own side of the road. In addition, force yourself to adjust speed on the presumption of troubles of the sort just described. It is best not to get *too* close in, however, because anyone coming in the other direction who is cutting the corner dangerously, doesn't then see you 'til a fraction later than he or she would otherwise; you also reduce your own room for manoeuvre. A balance has to be struck between all potential factors but you must always stick to your own side of the road. For a right hander, a course well in to your left greatly improves your vision into the bend.

Steering Through Slow Congested Traffic

This depends on judgment of gaps between vehicles, and competence must come by experience. During your first lesson or two it is well worth getting some old cardboard cartons and setting them up atop each other on an open space. Then drive SLOWLY past, as near to them as you can, both with the cartons on your own side of the car, and then with them on the passenger side. (You can stop whilst alongside to spy through the window just how near you have got.) Next, drive up to them, both forwards and in reverse, and stop close. See how near you can get without hitting them. Get out of the car to look and check your skill. Then set up pairs of cartons barely wider apart than the width of your car and drive through the gap. By doing this sort of thing you will learn to judge the width of your car without the possibility of damage. That will stand you in good stead when you start driving amongst traffic and wherever the road width has been narrowed by badly parked vehicles.

There is little more annoying than the driver who does not know the width of his car, and who therefore stops and holds up a

line of traffic instead of going through a perfectly adequate
space.

Use Of The Horn

Your car has a horn so that you can tell other road users that you
are there. It is a warning instrument, not a means of aggression.
Normally you hardly ever need it, and certainly you should
never drive "on the horn". Nevertheless, a hoot can save life; so
never flinch from giving one if circumstances demand it. While
passing through crowded shopping areas and other dangerous
places, it is always worth holding a finger at the ready to sound
your horn. Build this safety technique in during early days, it will
serve you well.

Headlight Flashing

The Highway Code decrees that headlights being flashed should
be regarded as having the same meaning as the sounding of a
horn, i.e. to signify the presence of the vehicle. You should
neither interpret nor use headlight flashing as a signal of
intention or of instruction. Despite the Code, some drivers flash
lights to mean "please come/go through", while others do the
SAME to mean "get out of the way – *I am* coming through,
FAST". Therefore you must make no assumptions when
headlight-flashers are about. Always hold back until you are
certain of their purpose. Beware also, of someone else suddenly
acting upon a signal you may have thought was intended for
you.

Headlights In Bad Daytime Visibility

The law states that you must put on headlights when visibility is
seriously reduced – whenever you cannot see beyond 100
metres. Whenever it is difficult to see, *or be seen,* because of bad
light, fog, snow, blizzard, hail, cloud or pelting rain, switch them
on. Use dipped beam.

7

RIGHT OF WAY AND TRAFFIC REGULATIONS

When asked, "When does a pedestrian have right of way?", nine out of ten drivers reply on the lines, "When on a zebra crossing"; "If a traffic light is at green for them"; or, "When a policeman holds back the traffic". The implied assumption is that, apart from such examples as were quoted, the pedestrian never has right of way.

How very wrong this is. If you give the matter thought, you will see that there is only one answer, *"Always"*.

Imagine driving along when a careless old man steps out into your path from behind a pillar-box. (If it's pelting rain, he'll probably dash out!) You cannot cut into the nearside because of the post-box; and in this case you cannot swerve out because of oncoming traffic.

What do you do? Unless you wish to find yourself in Court, you brake, with a view to stopping. Yes? Why? The pedestrian is not on a crossing. He is walking unconcernedly across a place where he has no right of way. Or has he? He most certainly has. You have given him right of way by virtue of the fact that you have stopped. He is not protected by his car. If you run him over, you probably won't hurt yourself, but you might kill him. That is why a pedestrian *always* has the right of way.

Right Of Way As Between One Vehicle And Another
With so many vehicles on the road, there have to be rules to determine which driver has right of way when their paths conflict. If failure to observe these rules results in an accident, the driver who had right of way will generally be held less to blame. The driver who did not have right of way will be wholly

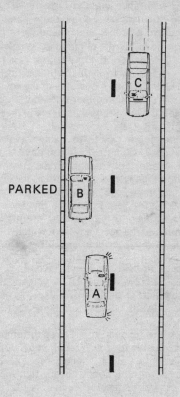

Fig. 8.   Right of way when there is a parked vehicle **B**.
Car **C** has right of way. If going on will cause car
C to have to slow down, car **A** must instead wait.
In car **C,** make no hasty assumptions; every car
A driver is not a saint! Sometimes, in car **C**, you
can move in to your nearside a little, thus
increasing the room car **A** then has for coming
through, sufficiently for him or her to do so
safely. When an opportunity presents itself, it is
good driving to help people in this way.

or mainly at fault. This is one of the things to be established when resolving insurance claims. Drivers who, when in the wrong, cause accidents, can also find themselves in Court. You must therefore have a proper understanding of right of way.

I repeat the basic U.K. rule of the road. **We drive on the left.** Leaving aside junctions for the moment, a general principle of right of way which follows from this, is that a car which is driving forwards on the left (i.e. on its own side of the road) has priority. A car which is overtaking another one and is on the "wrong" side, has no right of way, although it is free to do so if the road is clear.

The concept applies in exactly the same way if the car you are passing is stationary, as in fig. 8. If you have to wait, do so on your own side, comfortably back from the car you are going to have to pass round, and keeping parallel to the centre line. This avoids getting cramped up immediately behind the parked vehicle and having to cross the centre line by a much greater amount than necessary, when you do eventually go. It also means you command the best view from which to judge the right time to go. See Chapter 8 about signalling in this situation.

Narrow Lanes And "Single Track" Roads
Wherever a road is not wide enough for you and the fattest lorry to pass by each other, give and take is likely to be needed if you meet someone. Always wait for someone approaching, if you are in any doubt.

On country lanes, expect idiots at each blind corner. They whizz, carefree, unable to stop. You *must be slow*. At a corner, walking speed may be the maximum safe – and I advise you to give a well-timed warning hoot at every tight bend where you cannot see. When you do meet someone, the first thing to do is to slow or stop. One or other of you may then have to reverse before either can get through. The normal rule of the road is to give precedence to the driver going uphill: the downhill-facing person reverses. But use commonsense. If you are going uphill and have just passed a suitable place to pull into, it might be more sensible for you to back down. Usually one party stops as close to his left edge as possible whilst the other squeezes by. If a passing place has been provided, you dip into it, or wait opposite it, as appropriate. My advice to the "L" is always to let the other fellow do the squeezing past bit. At least if you are stopped, a scrape is less likely to be judged your fault!

Incidentally, never park in a single track road passing place;

that would be obstruction. People do it!

Narrow town streets with parking both sides are often just like single track roads. People use spaces between the parking as passing places and the same commonsense you would expect on a single track road.

"Give-Way" And "Stop" Signs

A "Give-way" or a "Stop" sign against you indicates that the road you are approaching is a major road, a more important road than the one you are on. Traffic on that major road has right of way. If you pull out on to the major road, forcing someone to swerve, or slow down, or causing an accident, you are in the wrong.

Every driver must stop at a "Stop" sign, BY LAW, regardless of whether the way is clear. You can go on immediately if there is no traffic, but you must make that stop first. "Stop" signs are rare, and only placed at junctions which are extremely dangerous. Stop when your front bumper reaches the solid line across the end of the road. Don't be fooled if a driver in front of you ignores the rules. Stop. You can lose your licence if you don't. Your examiner must fail you if you break a law.

At a junction with double broken "Give-Way" lines across the end of your road against you, you must still allow right of way to the major road traffic. You need not stop if the way is clear for you to join the major road but, again, you must not be the cause of any major-road driver having to slow or swerve, or of any accident.

Rights Along The Major Road

The "security" of having right of way along the major road is not sacrosanct. You cannot blast along expecting it to be clear. Crossing or turning traffic blocking it well before you arrive, or any other such blockage, however unpredictable, take precedence.

For example, if you smash into a herd of cows just beyond a blind bend, or ram into an accident that has already happened just over a hill brow, then by definition you will have been defying the Highway Code, and *driving so fast you could not stop well within the distance you could see to be clear.* You would be driving dangerously.

Note that a crossing/turning driver who has moved half-way out during a long gap from your direction (perhaps in despair of waiting instead for both directions to clear at once) and who has temporarily blanked off your lane before you arrive on the scene, is arguably within his or her rights. Although the Highway Code advises against any driver blocking any junction, you have no alternative in this event but to pull up, without anger, well short, so that the "offending" driver can best see no-one is trying to pass you, once he is able to complete his turn.

As an "L" you would not be expected to follow that driver's example, still less to be "pushy" about doing so, but there may be times you have to – with appropriate huge care; there can be danger from every direction. In the sense that major-road drivers tend to assume people won't do this sort of thing (an unrealistic assumption on today's crowded roads), there is always, in so doing, a degree of danger. In the event of a crash, a judge might well find against you (though in my view mistakenly, unless you gave someone no chance to stop), thus confirming right of way for those on the major road. The beak would probably have to do so anyway, were there to be any doubt about the distance over which the major-road driver should easily have been aware you were blocking the lane.

Traffic Lights
In busy places these change right of way alternately between one road and another. Each one becomes the major road in turn. You only have right of way through a traffic light when the light shows green for you. Similarly, where a policeman or traffic warden is controlling traffic at a junction, you only have right of way when the officer beckons or is holding all the crossing traffic at a stop. But it is your look-out! Not that of the officer. Even if beckoned forward (or at a green light), you are still obliged to look out for pedestrians and stray vehicles. You cannot run people down, no matter how "wrong" they might be.

If when you are free to go forward at traffic-light or police-controlled junctions, you are also *turning* (right or left), notice that pedestrians crossing the neck of the road you are to enter, will be correct to expect to be able to do so without hindrance. Be prepared to wait for them. You dare not risk hitting anybody in any event, but here, right of way changes immediately you begin to turn. Whereas the green light, or the policeman's instructions, remain in the pedestrian's favour, they are now no longer in yours.

Box Junctions
Because of traffic congestion, many traffic lights and other junctions now have criss-cross yellow lines painted across the

entire area. The concept (and the rule) is that you hold back from entering the criss-crossed part (even if a green light shows for you) until you can see space for you beyond it. The only exception, for which you may enter the painted area and allow yourself to have to stop within it, is if you are turning right and will only have to wait in there because of oncoming vehicles to which you must give way.

If someone fails to follow these rules and blocks you when you could have been going, or when lights change in your favour, the existence of the rules does not give you any greater right of way – annoying as it is! It would be wonderful if ALL drivers treated ALL junctions on the box junction basis. And if they did so, not just where major roads meet, but equally when they were in a queue on a major road and adjacent to any side turning. Is it too much to hope for such a utopian virtue to become universal within our driving lifespan?!

Zebra Crossings

Sometimes these crossings are additionally controlled by a policeman, traffic warden or "lollipop" person. In that case you must obey the controller's directions. But remember it will be your look-out should the controller make a mistake and beckon you into danger.

On uncontrolled zebra crossings, the moment a pedestrian places a foot on the crossing (or moves a pram out, etc.) YOU MUST STOP, BY LAW. Only if you could prove stopping would have caused an accident would you have much chance in Court if you had been reported going through. If you hit a pedestrian, you would then have, I guess, no chance!

If a pedestrian is standing on the kerb or in the centre island of a zebra crossing, then you do not *in law* have to stop. But you must be ready to stop in case that person steps out suddenly. It is more courteous, and very often more sensible, to stop anyway, and let him or her cross.

Always try to stop gently and several metres short of the zebra lines themselves. There is a broken "official" give-way line about one metre short, but I believe it is better not to go right up to that mark. My way, gives pedestrians peace of mind, and a better chance for them to spot those loony law-breakers who try to shoot past you. (Motorcyclists frequently do it!) Use your handbrake and come out of gear. As soon as the last pedestrian clears you can go. Leave a reasonable time after that person has passed so as not to frighten anyone. Only then take 1st gear; this removes any risk of endangering a pedestrian through an inadvertent lurch forward.

For the protection of pedestrians, stringent rules exist to prevent overtaking on the approach to zebra crossings. Zig-zag white lines are marked alongside the kerb and in the centre of the road, both before, and after the crossing. IT IS ILLEGAL to overtake the leading vehicle (i.e. the one nearest to the crossing) once you are within the zig-zag marked area. You may not overtake either on its outside or its inside. It makes no difference whether it is stopping, has stopped, or has no need to. Nor does it matter whether or not there are pedestrians on or around the crossing. The law on this is absolute.

If there are two lanes on the approach to the crossing, then you may stop *alongside* the leading vehicle. Once you have done so, however, there seems no part of the rule to say you should not move ahead side by side, if, by then, the crossing has cleared; nor does there appear to be any requirement to wait if the original leading car is then held longer than you, or is slow to get on when it can, though personally I would not try to be too clever. These are fine points, no doubt liable one day to be tested in Court.

In queueing conditions, leave zebras clear. Do not stop on them, making life awkward for walkers.

Pelican Crossings

These traffic-light-controlled crossings for pedestrians save undue delay for drivers by substituting flashing amber for the normal red plus amber phase of junction traffic lights. Treat the other phases as you would normal traffic lights, i.e. Red STOP! Green GO with care! Steady AMBER – STOP! unless you cannot do so safely.

The flashing AMBER stage which follows red allows you to go as soon as the crossing clears. You GIVE WAY to any pedestrians, but once the last one has passed, you move on even if green has yet to appear. The signal facing the pedestrians during this phase is a flashing on/off green man warning them not to start crossing as the lights are about to change; the bleep, bleep which informs blind people they may walk across safely also stops.

You should be alert, ready for stopping, if people are on foot near a pelican. Even if they have crossed already before steady amber and then red come on, you must still STOP. On dual carriageways you will often see drivers overtaking through green pelicans despite people standing waiting. The Highway Code warns you not to do this; hold back 'til after. For practical purposes the best drivers treat arriving at pelicans as if zig-zag rules applied. (Many of them have zig-zag lines painted in any case.) When first to have to stop, they never frighten pedestrians by rushing up to the stop line, or disturb walkers by impatient blipping of the accelerator whilst they are waiting. As at a zebra, they await the last biped before engaging 1st gear.

Roundabouts

Generally, traffic coming from the right – that which is already on the roundabout – has right of way over traffic entering. Exceptions are rare but in a few places broken "give-way" lines across the roundabout lanes dictate otherwise. Apart from these, you are, therefore, invariably in the wrong if you collide with a vehicle that comes from your right on a roundabout.

Lane Changing

In Chapter 6 I referred to keeping in the middle of whichever lane you are in when there are several from which to choose. People *also expect* that you will STAY IN LANE, unless you signal an intended change.

A lane change to left or right demands a flashing indicator signal if anyone else could conceivably be affected. (Sometimes that will include people ahead as well as behind.) If you are moving lanes prior to making a turn, you will be wanting your flashing indicator anyway; it just needs to begin earlier, before the preparatory lane-change, and then remain on. If you are only changing lane, for example to pass round roadworks or because someone in front is going to turn right, a brief signal is all you need.

Part of continually watching *far* ahead, also stressed in Chapter 6, will be spotting when you will require to swap lanes. It is this anticipation that gives you the chance to pick the right moment. It provides the time to watch your mirrors so that you can see your signal is "accepted" by those behind, before you move smoothly across.

Sometimes, when traffic in the next lane is heavy, you will find speeding up to move ahead of someone is the appropriate thing because you can see that's what he or she is expecting (but look out in front!); more usually you would slow a little and move in behind.

If your appropriate left or right flashing indicator is only for a lane change, not for a specific turn you are shortly going to make, remember to cancel it directly you are in the new lane. (See page 70.)

Mirrors are not always quite enough with which to survey behind before lane changes, if traffic is heavy. You need to confirm, with a glance over the appropriate shoulder, that no-one has been hidden close behind in a blind spot (see fig. 31).

In terms of right of way, you ought never to force anyone behind to have to slow or brake, still less swerve, in order to let you move over. However, whenever someone wants to come in front of you, let him, or her, in. There may be life-saving urgency unseen by you; and there is simple courtesy...

Sometimes, if you are too late for a lane change and there is no sign of whoever is behind giving you a late chance, you simply have to forget it; do whatever those in your present lane are doing, and sort yourself out later. Do not just come to an abrupt halt in the middle of a fast road!

Chapter 11 on overtaking highlights some more lane changing snags.

Reversing

It is illegal to reverse further than necessary. While reversing, you *never* have precedence. If anyone comes in your way, STOP. Let them pass; move forward if this will help. Remember, pedestrians can be pint-sized (i.e. children). Get out and look first if you have the slightest doubt that the ground is clear behind.

Traffic Regulations

These could fill an entire book with a mass of legal jargon. However, the major ones are all spelled out in the Highway Code. You must understand them, despite the gobbledegook which you will find even in there. Below, for your information, I give a general list of the main offences for which the law can clamp down upon you. The list must only be regarded as a guide, since Acts of Parliament are subject to frequent change; new offences are added, or old ones are re-defined. The latest position therefore always requires to be checked.

Causing death by driving dangerously.
Driving at dangerous speed or in a dangerous way, or without due care and attention, or without reasonable consideration for

other road users.

Obstruction by parking, or dangerous parking.

Parking without lights at night, other than where allowed.

Disobeying a policeman's, traffic warden's, or school crossing patrol's, signal, or a traffic light, or a mandatory sign.

Crossing a double white line where there is a continuous line on the side nearest your vehicle.

Driving or attempting to drive, or being in charge of, a motor vehicle, with more than 80 milligrams of alcohol in 100 millilitres of your blood, or, with more than 35 micrograms of alcohol per 100 millilitres of your breath, as measured by breathalyser. (Up to the 50 microgram level, you have the option of taking a blood or urine test to confirm or disprove a breath test.)

Driving under the influence of a drug.

Driving with uncorrected defective eyesight.

Driving an unlicenced or uninsured vehicle, or whilst you are disqualified.

Driving with faulty steering, or brakes, or with defective tyres.

Driving with your flashing direction indicators out of order.

Driving without a horn; hooting while stationary unless in danger, or between 11.30 p.m. and 7 a.m. in built-up areas.

Failing to stop after an accident and give particulars to anyone reasonably requiring them.

Driving without a licence, failing to sign your driving licence in ink, or failing to notify your change of address to the authority.

Driving without "L" plates, or unaccompanied, before passing your Test.

Failing to produce your certificate of insurance and your vehicle M.O.T. certificate (if appropriate), when required, or, instead, to present them within seven days at any police station.

Opening a car door dangerously. (This includes danger to *pedestrians...*).

Breakdowns And "Warning Triangles"

These triangles are worth keeping in the car. In the event of any accident or breakdown obstructing the road, they should be placed well back (the legal minimum is 50 metres), and by the road edge, so as to warn further traffic from behind.

Always get off the road, if possible, should you break down. On a "fast" road you are in considerable danger. Push the car or drive it "on the starter" in 1st gear (not possible with automatic transmission). If you cannot get clear of the road, use the hazard warning four-way flashers, and at night, sidelights too; open the bootlid or tail door, and leave the back seat squab or some large object leaning up against the middle of the back bumper where it won't obscure your lights. This will alert traffic from behind that your car is stuck. Open the bonnet so that approaching traffic is warned too. Keep children and animals under control, and if there is any danger that your vehicle could be smashed into, take your passengers to a place of safety, off the road, away from the car.

8

SIGNALLING

A turn signal only warns other road users what you intend to do. It does not give you the right to do it. You first have to check that your way is clear, and that you will not endanger any other road user.

Remember the Highway Code dictum: **Mirrors – Signal – Manoeuvre.** The examiner will notice whether you remember that the mirrors-check must always be before your signal.

Test examiners recognise that for turns flashing indicators are best. This is mainly because arm signals are less easily seen by day and hopelessly difficult to see by night. (See also fig. 9.) You are therefore not normally asked to give arm *turn* signals as you drive on your Test. Nevertheless, examiners want to ensure both that you can recognise the correct arm turn signals, and that you could use them yourself if necessary, as in the case of a sudden failure of your flashing indicators, or for telling a policeman or traffic warden the way you want to go. So you can still expect to be asked questions about the arm turn signals, or to have to demonstrate any of them, though probably not with the car on the move.

The Highway Code points out that you can always reinforce a flashing indicator signal with an arm signal. This might be very useful, for example, on a very bright sunny day when flashing indicators show up less well.

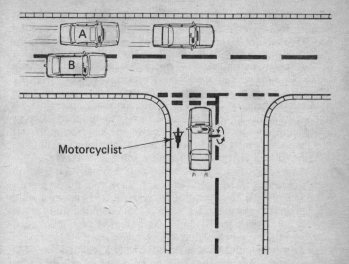

Motorcyclist

Fig. 9. Unseen arm turn signal. In this picture, **A** and **B**, and the motorcyclist, cannot see the signal at all! **B**, passing at the junction, is driving *dangerously,* breaking the Highway Code rule "You **MUST NOT** overtake...at a road junction."

At roundabouts, flashing indicators are the only viable signals. The special care needed with their timing is best studied in conjunction with roundabout lane discipline and therefore I have incorporated them into Chapter 10.

Flashing Indicator Signals
In fig. 9, apart from the problem of the arm turn signal being hidden, the driver shown turning left is appallingly positioned. The car is too far out, which has encouraged the motorcyclist to risk moving up on the inside. And, because the driver has not begun to point the car to the left even though it's almost at the line, the way it is placed on the road reveals no clue as to where that driver wants to go. As a car driver making a left turn of this sort, you must learn to hug the kerb both as you position and when you come to pull out. Then everyone should know what

you're up to. Nevertheless, even though having checked your mirrors earlier, you still need a final double-check over your shoulder too, to be sure you cannot squash anyone on two wheels who might be trying to get up alongside. Such a person may be foolish and in breach of the Highway Code rules, but it's best to let that be; you dare not risk knocking over a two-wheeler, who is so much more vulnerable than you are.

In contrast, an articulated lorry cannot always hug the kerb like a car should do. That has to leave substantial room so as to avoid battering the kerb. So never move up alongside on the left of a heavy wagon at any junction unless you know it cannot be wanting to turn left; wait 'til you are sure!

Flashing indicator turn signals should normally be given in plenty of time; that is, just after you check in your mirrors, prior to taking up the correct position for your turn. Then they should stay on until the turn is completed. A more detailed study of the correct timing for signals at turns, traffic lights and roundabouts, comes in the next two chapters.

The flashing indicator is designed to self-cancel; it does so the very next time you turn the wheel by any material amount in the opposite direction to that in which you have the indicator set. Thus it should cancel itself as you straighten up after your turn. If your turn is only slight, however, it may not cancel itself automatically. Therefore develop a habit of checking, after every turn, that the control stalk has flipped back. Spread the habit to those times when you have signalled for changing lane, or for moving off (signals you should always do!), because then you don't turn the steering very much but the car doesn't know you are not going to... How annoying it is to follow a fellow whose indicator is still flashing away merrily when its use is finished. This can be the cause of a serious accident. Such a forgetful driver, you should note, is in any case likely to turn in any direction without remembering to change that signal.

Another serious mistake which learners, unfamiliar with the multiple nature of the flashing indicator control stalk, are apt to make, is to inadvertently flash their headlights (by pulling the stalk towards themselves), whilst trying to indicate left or right. The danger of such a mistaken headlights flash being misinterpreted was highlighted at the end of Chapter 6.

To give a turn signal too soon can sometimes be as great a mistake as to give it too late. Imagine you are on a major road which has many intersecting turnings. If you intend to turn off into a road which may be three or four intersections away, you

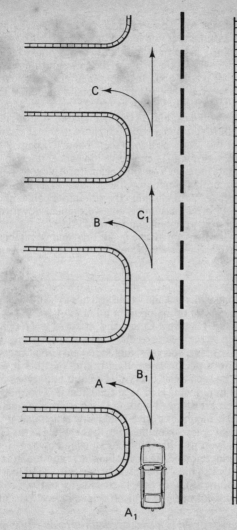

Fig. 10. When to signal. Driver turning down road **A** would signal from **A₁**, going down road **B** – would not begin to signal until **B₁**, or until **C₁**, for going down road **C**.

must not signal too soon because other drivers may then mistakenly assume that you intend turning at the first junction, and not the third, or perhaps fourth, as you may have in mind. A driver waiting to come out of one of the earlier turnings may pull out right in front of you. In this situation, you must delay signalling until you have passed the road next-before the one you are going to turn into. See fig. 10. If you were coming the opposite way to the car in fig. 10, and intending to turn right into other than the first turning, you would have to signal and take up a "crown of the road" position (see Chapter 9, page 90) well before the first turning. Then you would cancel the signal until the appropriate moment to begin it again, to be judged finely, just as in the left turning situation. Otherwise, a driver exiting from road B to turn right, might jump the gun into a collision course with you, that driver assuming you were going down road C, when in fact you were heading for road A!

Notice that when you meet a major road and you intend to go straight ahead as soon as it is safe for you to cross it, you give no flashing indicators at any stage.

Arm Signals

As "arm" signal implies, the whole arm has to be used. They are not "hand" signals drooping from a limp wrist.

Look in the Highway Code, and at fig. 11. Notice three things:

1. That there is a special signal to indicate your intention of turning left to a person controlling traffic, but that it will not necessarily be seen by followers. Therefore both types may be needed at different stages. The special signal is normally only for use if you are stopped waiting at the front of a queue.

2. That it is incorrect to give a slow-down signal at any stage of turning right or left, or pulling in to the nearside kerb. The turn signal which you use, itself implies slowing down.

3. As distinct from using no flashing indicator for straight on, there *is* an arm signal – to be given when it is useful to confirm where you want to go, to people controlling traffic.

To be learned properly all the arm signals need to be put into practice.

They must be given in a concise, definite and distinct way, in plenty of time, and with as much of your arm out of the window as you can comfortably and safely manage.

In the case of arm *turn* signals, this need not mean using them every time you go out, but they must be tried at least on one or

To vehicles behind.	To a policeman or traffic warden, or anyone ahead.

I am going to turn left or move in to the left, or pull in to the nearside kerb.

I am going to turn right or move out.

I am going straight on.

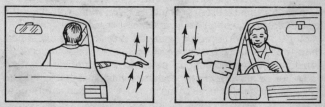

I am going to slow down or I am going to stop.

Fig. 11. Correct arm signals.

two occasions during your lessons. They must always be accompanied by the appropriate flashing indicator (unless that is temporarily broken). The slow-down arm signal needs practice in all your later lessons, because, quite rightly, you are still expected to give it *on Test*, whenever an appropriate occasion arises.

An arm turn signal should not be unduly prolonged. It must be completed well before you reach the junction, because you must have both hands on the steering wheel whilst going round.

Add your arm turn signal during the third gear stage as you prepare for the turn. This should be about 75 metres before it, as discussed in Chapter 9; however, if you are going slowly, a little later may be best. You can help yourself to ample time for the arm turn signal by making your change to 3rd a little earlier than normal. In practice, you have to do that, because the gear change and arm signal cannot be done simultaneously. That would mean letting go of the wheel completely and that would mean Test failure because you must never take both hands off the wheel at once!

There is normally no need to repeat an arm turn signal. One clear-cut arm turn signal is usually sufficient. However, if you have given the signal prior to arriving at some traffic lights, and then you have been held up at the lights, give a further signal before setting off again at green. Traffic conditions will have changed over the length of time you have waited, and there may, by then, be other road users around who have yet to become aware of your intended turn.

The Slow-Down Signal

When you are in a traffic stream which has been flowing nicely, you should try to use a "slow-down" signal if you all have to slow or stop. The most important times are when you are at the front of a stream, or will be the first member of it who has to slow or stop. It can be especially good driving at traffic lights or a pedestrian crossing, because other people in the situation who might be affected (coming the other way for example) may not notice, or be able to see, the reason for the stopping. Give it as soon as you have checked your mirrors and changed into 3rd gear (see pages 46 and 49). Examiners do like to see the "slow-down" signal given when traffic conditions merit its use. Your brakelights automatically alert the people behind, but the arm signal adds emphasis. It can also confirm to pedestrians that you are stopping for them.

Imagine driving briskly along the open road when some unexpected obstruction crops up. You are going to have to stop quickly although it won't be an "emergency stop". You can leave out changing down the gears if you have to, but do try to use a "slow-down" arm signal *if time permits,* and flash your brakelights on and off at the start of your braking (again, only if there is time), so that they awaken drivers behind to the fact that there is something unexpected happening. Remember that many drivers go along in a daydream, gazing at the scenery and thinking lovely thoughts. That is the cause of many of the "concertina" type crashes. Their eyes are open but they are wide asleep. After any sudden stop, keep your brakelights flashing until you can see people behind have reacted.

Pulling In To The Nearside (Left Side) To Stop By The Kerb

Always use your left flashing indicator. Start it after you have checked your mirrors before beginning to slow down, and at least 75 metres ahead of where you intend to stop. Take 3rd gear to help you slow; as you are stopping, there is no need for any further downward change. Cancel the signal once stopped.

A left turn arm signal can sometimes add to safety by confirming your flashing indicator. It prevents drivers behind from failing to appreciate you are stopping. Even if they didn't notice you start your indicator, they can then hardly imagine that you might have left it flashing by mistake.

On Test, the examiner asks you to pull up at the left side of the road from time to time. When the request is phrased for you to, "stop on the left when you can", you are expected to select the next safe spot, taking account of parking rules (see Chapter 12), and of its suitability with regard to other traffic. (You would for example, I hope, never attempt to pull in so close to a turning that your car might block people's view! – not to mention that the Highway Code states you mustn't even wait, never mind park, within 15 metres of a junction!) When the examiner wants you to reverse into a limited opening – a Test manoeuvre described in Chapter 12 – he or she will be specific about where you are to pull in. It will be nearby to the opening chosen although a safe distance away from it. As the opening will, more often than not, be one to the left the examiner will also be watching to see that you time your signal for pulling in, carefully, so that nobody else can mistake your intention of stopping *after* the turning, rather than going into it. (See fig. 10.)

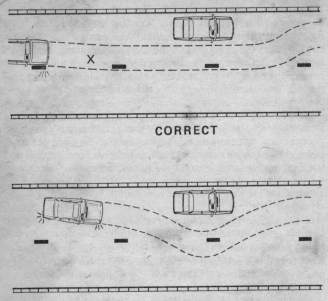

CORRECT

WRONG

Fig. 12. Passing a parked vehicle. The top half of this picture shows the **CORRECT** path: moving out is
begun well back and no signal is strictly necessary.
At the point you are alongside the parked car, you
are parallel to it. You move in smoothly immediately
the vehicle has been passed. If you can see you are
going to have to stop to give way to approaching
traffic (as is presumed here although there isn't
room to show it), put on your right flashing indicator
well before you stop. Keep it on 'til you go. Wait at
point X; otherwise you will find yourself too close to
the parked car, and then having to fall into the error
of an acute swing out afterwards.

The bottom half of the picture shows the **WRONG**
way – with an unnecessarily sharp swing out, too
late. Note that had this driver positioned correctly
his signal might have been unnecessary.

Your stop may be preparatory to reversing into a parking space (see page 142) amongst a long line of parked cars. Left flashing indicator tells people behind you want to pull in, but a left turn arm signal given as well, draws their attention better. Hopefully, if they cannot pass straightaway, they will stop far enough back from you to let you do your initial reverse inwards.

Passing A Parked Vehicle Or Roadworks

Learners often signal their intention to overtake a parked vehicle regardless of circumstances. It is necessary if a wide detour is being made, but is frequently not needed if you are not going to have to stop, and if your car is positioned in plenty of time ready for the overtake. You should be able to anticipate well ahead, check your mirrors, and bear out gradually; see fig. 12. Do signal if a driver behind is very close or "threatening" to pass you. Do signal – from well in advance – if you *will* have to stop. Keep it on while waiting. Cancel it as you set off.

It is better always to signal for small obstructions at night – or whenever those behind are less likely to be able to see what the problem is – but never prolong a signal of this kind. Drivers behind may think you are going to turn right.

Remember that, depending on room, *you* stop to give right of way to approaching traffic when a car or obstruction is on your side of the road. When the obstruction is on the other side the opposite should apply. But I'm afraid you are going to meet some diabolical drivers who try to "barge" through, when it is they who should stop. Assume nothing. Be prepared to stop yourself until you see that they are going to.

Sometimes, if you are to be obliged to stop on a steep uphill, drivers coming down will courteously choose to stop for you instead. Don't depend on it! However, in the converse situation, show kindness and wait – saving them having to face a stiff uphill start.

The Moving Off Signal When Pulling Out From The Kerb

Occasionally, when a road is entirely clear, you can dispense with a moving off signal; however most places nowadays are always sufficiently busy for a signal to be helpful to someone, whether they appear behind just as you move, or they are coming the other way, or you have failed to notice them... Therefore, a good personal rule is always to include right flashing indicator; part two of this rule is to remember the cancel habit immediately you are going! (See page 70).

The time to begin this signal is when you release the handbrake (Step 6 of the Smooth Take-Off). Then, with the handbrake off and holding the car steady under clutch control (see Chapter 2 – or Chapter 13 if you have automatic transmission), you must check specifically that there is nothing approaching from behind. Look in your mirrors (which you may have been able to do already). Confirm what you see there, *by turning your head round to look* over your right shoulder. Once everything is going to be clear behind for a decent length of time, look in front again and get going smartly if it is still safe. **N.B.1:** A common and potentially dangerous learners' mistake is to begin creeping forward whilst still looking backwards. Don't! Suppose someone has walked in front of you! **N.B.2:** Whilst turning your head to the front again, be sure to look out for anyone stepping out from either side smack in front of your bonnet. That too, is a favourite, if unbelievable, form of pedestrian madness.

With heavy passing traffic, and, maybe, pedestrians about, you often have to return to "square one" of this combined Smooth Take-Off and looking process, perhaps several times, before a chance comes up to move off safely with everything clear at once. How to handle the gears and clutch in this event was explained in Step 6, page 23. Cancel your flashing indicator meantime; start it afresh when you come to release the handbrake again.

Fig. 13 illustrates a common accident, when the additional problem of getting out from behind a parked car both tempts a driver to depend on mirrors alone, and causes him or her to forget to signal. Driver number 2 is going happily along when number 1 (often a van or lorry) pulls out without having looked directly behind over the right shoulder. Number 2 swings out to avoid number 1 and hits number 3. Someone is probably killed. If number 1 had physically checked over his or her shoulder this would not have happened.

Wherever you come to a parked vehicle which could have a driver in it, you dare not take it for granted that that driver is aware that you are coming – that the person concerned will not swing out from the kerb unexpectedly. Observant drivers try never to get into a situation where such untimely action by another driver could cause an accident. They leave a minimum of one door's opening width between themselves and any stopped vehicle.

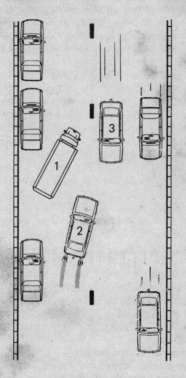

Fig. 13. A very common accident.

which they are passing. They also cut their own speed down
sufficiently to be able to take evasive action or stop if necessary
– either if it does happen, if a door is opened carelessly, or if
hidden children dash out from behind the vehicle after a ball, etc.
And where there is a line of parked vehicles they exercise even
more care. They know that to swing out as number 2 did *puts
them in the wrong too,* never mind the danger. Two wrongs don't
(re)make a life.

Emergencies such as those just described DO HAPPEN!

Control your speed according to the adequateness of the space you are able to leave. If oncoming traffic restricts your room, and/or your vision, you must accept the discipline of Commandment 9, Chapter 17. Give yourself a chance; don't take them.

You can increase your chances for safety, as you approach any such stationary vehicle, if you watch for any tell-tale signs that it might pull out – brakelights going off, driver's window winding down...etc. A hoot is appropriate to warn the driver of your presence. If you see someone preparing to go, train yourself to glance at the vehicle's offside front wing and wheel. Movement there is usually the first to show, and it's proof!

9

LEFT AND RIGHT TURNS

Turning at road junctions causes the major proportion of accidents. Right turns are worst because of the added risk of conflict with other road users whose paths need to be crossed.

Going In Front Of Other People

Every time you pull out on to a major road, cross it, or turn right off it, your movements could conflict with those of other drivers who have right of way.

The acid test, which you must always ask yourself before going, is – will any such person already coming along the major road be forced to slow down? If they will, do not go! The Highway Code rule is that you must never cause anyone to have to slow down. Wait, unless the only others involved are clearly waiting for you – confirmed by seeing beyond doubt that they are stopping.

It follows that when you cross someone's right of way even in good time, you must be certain you can get clear in one go. You cannot suddenly stop half-way. Therefore two things must *always* apply: (1) the space beyond their path, for which you are heading, must be free for you. (Remember that pedestrians might – within their rights, *or not* – wander on to it, or into your way before you get there.) (2) you must know that your car will get you to that space whatever happens.

Sometimes you will be approaching a turning or crossing point and will judge that your momentum will anyway assure you of that latter safety. In other positions you will have already had to stop, either because the layout and road markings legally oblige you to, or because you are going to need to wait for a gap in a stream of traffic anyway. The danger then will be of stalling the engine when you do go.

Always make double-sure that you are giving sufficient acceleration, without "roaring" the engine, to enable you to get across another person's right of way without any risk of stalling. Adequate engine revs must be maintained before releasing the clutch. Be extra careful if the engine is still warming up under choke. See that you do not engage 3rd gear in mistake for 1st – or forget to release the handbrake. All these are simple matters...of life or death.

Never go on unless you are certain that you could reach safety at walking speed, still without inconveniencing any other road user. Never commit yourself to going if you are in any doubt about the potential action of another road user.

Suppose that you have stalled and are stuck half-away across someone's right of way. Sometimes, by the time your engine is re-started, it will no longer be safe to try to go forward; indeed, you must try quickly to reverse out of danger. O.K. – if some idiot has not moved up on you behind! People behind you should *never* do that before being sure you are safely out or across. But you dare not rely on it that they won't. I have to promise you that many of them cannot think beyond their noses.

Letting Other People Go

Whenever someone else is going across your right of way, ease your speed until you see they are going to make it.

It takes two to make an accident! Countless smashes would be avoided if major road pigheads resolved always to *be prepared* for stopping. Have your foot over the brake, ready. Keep awake; stay alive! Remind yourself that someone straddled across your lane since long before you come within striking distance, does have a "right", conferred by the circumstances being appropriate, to sit there until able to move on. That "right" is virtually equal to your "right" to be coming along. See Chapter 7: **Your Rights Along The Major Road.**

Eagle Eyes At Junctions

When it is your right of way past a turning or through a crossroads, it is also your divine right to be on the look-out for trouble, and to control speed 'til it is clear that no person or vehicle can possibly shoot out in front of you, or in front of oncoming traffic which might then finish up on your side. No-one else will do it for you. Scan, scan and scan again as you reach these hazards, but never forgetting to *look ahead* in case the driver immediately in front of you is stopping – or lest drivers further ahead of him have begun to pull up unexpectedly. Traffic lights at green for you are no excuse for less diligence in watching all directions, especially if pedestrians are afoot.

Joining Major Roads

When you are emerging on to or crossing a major road, you need a specific drill for looking right and left, *thoroughly*. At crossroads you have to take account of what anyone opposite may do too, even if you are only turning left (they may try to swing across ahead of you). You must also retain a healthy distrust of any drivers displaying a flashing indicator signal, until their *actions* confirm it. This particularly applies to those coming along a major road, signalling left to enter a minor road you are leaving. They may have forgotten to cancel their flashing indicator from some time before, and have no such intention, or they may simply change their minds. Wait until you are sure what they are up to, and are certain nothing hidden behind them (such as a motor scooter) might be put at risk if you move.

In the old days, when you arrived at a major road, the adage *"look right, left, and right again"* for traffic, served reasonably well. But it forgot to emphasise that you must scan the pavements FIRST, as you arrive, for pedestrians.

That basic adage still stands but you need a bit more cunning. Tips that will boost your looking efficiency are given all through this book; learn them well; they are life-savers.

Restricted Vision Junctions

A major road entry point with restricted right/left vision because of buildings, high grassy banks, or whatever, is not an excuse for your front bumper to stick out over the line into the major road before you can see. If no line is painted, as may be the case in side streets or country lanes, you must imagine where it would extend across from gutter to gutter, or edge of road to edge of road. In these circumstances you often have to stop (or take 1st gear still just on the move) *before* the end, and then nose your bumper up to the line looking all the while. By edging forwards gingerly for the last metre or two, you can almost always gain the view you need. You can do so in safety, ready to stop instantly if required, and without the front of your car crossing the line of the outside pavement edge. That view gained, you can stop if necessary (or if a "stop" sign/line commands you must anyway), whilst you complete *looking right, left, and right again,* repeating the process until you are certain your way is clear. Lean forward. It helps you see. Open your window(s). Then you hear (traffic coming).

Should you ever have no choice but partly to cross that line before you can see properly, always be looking right, at the critical moment of crossing it (or left if it's a one-way street with traffic coming from the left). In other words, be looking in the direction from which the major road traffic is likely to be passing closest to your bonnet.

Open Vision Junctions

There is usually a give-way sign and/or lines on the road at the entry to a major road wherever right/left vision is open and good. If there are no markings, treat the junction in the same way but with enormous extra care. You are legally free to join the major road without a stop ONLY if all is clear.

It is important to avoid an unnecessary stop. That will only serve to annoy drivers following you. In order to decide whether you need to stop or not, your looking drill has to be advanced into your final approach to a greater extent, but there must be no less attention to detail. If you have not had enough time to satisfy yourself it is safe, you must stop, regardless of people behind. If you are going to be second to arrive, expect that the driver ahead may do just that, even if *you* can already see the road is clear. Never assume that driver will have been looking as skilfully as you may be doing; suppose the person has decided to stop anyway, to re-adjust his or her seatbelt...! Crash-Bang-Wallop!

Many minor shunts occur in this way. Indeed, at the entry points to roundabouts this is the most popular error which learners – and their supposedly qualified peers – make. Remember, that at all such junction points where you hope to keep on the move, other traffic permitting, looking *where you are going* must take equal place with checking right and left.

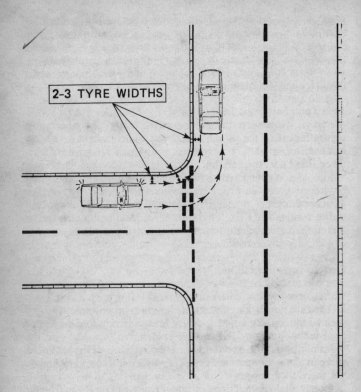

2-3 TYRE WIDTHS

Fig. 14. Correct path for a left turn on to a major road.

Get Going!

Once YOU (not the examiner, your instructor, or anyone else) are satisfied a major road is clear to give you ample time to get on and go, do so smartly. Waiting when you need not, may be seen as "undue hesitancy", a driving fault.

Never creep partly out into a major road. Moving out and blocking the entire half of it nearest to you is sometimes indulged in by non-learners, as described on page 61. Then the traffic coming from the right has to stop. But if you ease partly out, they are squeezed, putting themselves, and anyone correctly positioned waiting to turn right off the major road (in *either* direction), in unnecessary danger. This is particularly deadly at night, when drivers don't spot what's happening in time. It would also serve you right if you were hit by a major-road driver from your left, cutting across whilst turning right. See fig. 20.

Left Turn Joining a Major Road
When you take a left turn on to a major road, you join directly the traffic stream travelling nearest to you, from right to left. As has been explained, provided there is a gap for you to move into, there is no necessity to stop at the junction, unless there is a "stop" sign, or there are traffic lights at red against you. You only need to stop if anyone coming from the right is too near for your safe exit – or if anyone from the left is overtaking dangerously and encroaching on your side of the road. Forget to watch for the latter idiot at your peril. See fig. 15.

This left turn should be taken as follows: Approximately 75 metres before the junction, check your mirrors carefully, then signal your intention (see page 68) and slip into 3rd gear. Take up the correct position for the turn, which is within 2-3 tyre widths from the nearside kerb. See fig. 14. If giving an arm signal in addition to your flashing indicator, do it as soon as you have taken 3rd. Brake gently to reduce speed as required.

If you can see you are going to have to stop because the junction is "blind", or if there is a "stop" sign and line anyway, there is no need to drop to 2nd. Remain in 3rd and stop when you get there.

Watch that no-one steps off the pavement(s) right in front of you just as you reach the line. Begin looking both ways as soon as the view opens up. (Remember to look the correct way first – see page 83!) Once stopped, apply the handbrake, return the gear to neutral, release the clutch pedal; be prepared for a full smooth take-off in 1st gear when ready.

Repeat your *look right, left, and right again* procedure until you are certain you are safe to go. Then, with a final glance across your left shoulder, if necessary, to be sure no cyclist has crept up on your left to be allowed for, go – smartly. Make a habit to check your mirrors as you straighten up – so that you are straightaway on to the mirrors' picture for your new road. Accelerate up through the gears without delay, so as to match traffic speed for the faster road. Unless major road traffic is being held up, dawdle not; you could get hit from behind.

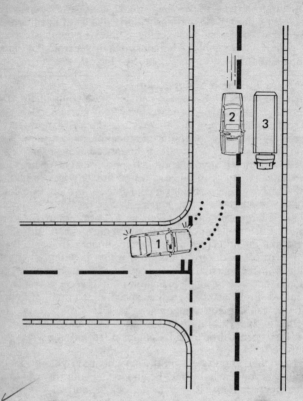

Fig. 15. Danger of an overtaking vehicle when turning left. Driver no. **1** must check carefully to his or her *left,* and be awake to the danger of a car like no. **2**, overtaking lorry no. **3**, or there will be a serious accident. The fact that no. **2** should be put in jail for even considering attempting to overtake at a junction, does not, regrettably, make this problem on our roads go away.

With good open views both ways on the approach, and "give-way" markings, you *do* drop down into 2nd gear about 25-30 metres from the junction, and to about 10 m.p.h. by the time you have 10-15 metres left to go.

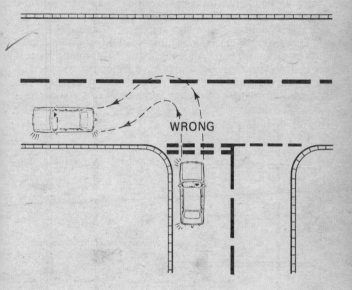

Fig. 16. Swinging out at a left turn. **WRONG.**

You begin your looking left and right drill from as early on as the unfolding scene allows. Remember that the pavements, and all the other potential snags we have mentioned so far, have all got to be looked for on the move, so having that speed right down is essential. Control of your speed is also vital, so that a last-second decision to stop at the line is easy to make if you have to. Of course, it may be obvious from early on that you will have to stop. In either event, you simply stop at the line, and then prepare at once for carrying out the full procedure – just described above – as soon as it is safe to go.

If, on the other hand, the major road remains clear, or you can

see that a convenient safe gap in the traffic will coincide with
your arrival, then, being in 2nd gear, you have got the
acceleration/power to get on and go ahead without a stop. You
do so in that case, getting smartly on your way, and up to an
appropriate speed for the major road.

Very occasionally, at a wide, sweeping "give-way" junction
with unobstructed vision, if all is clear, you can go ahead in 3rd
gear at 15-20 m.p.h. (a rough maximum for proper safety)
without needing to change down to 2nd at all. Most junctions,
however, dictate 10 m.p.h. or less and 2nd gear, because space is
confined, and the chance you may have to stop remains right up
to the very last moment. (2nd ensures adequate power and
eliminates any danger of stalling in the event that you can go.)

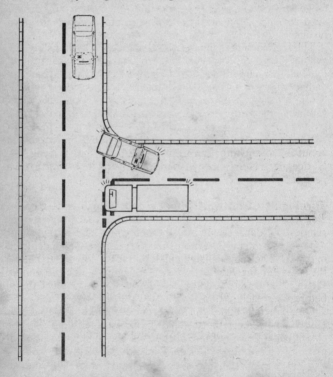

Fig. 17. Mounting the pavement by mistake.

Blind Spots

I have stressed that when emerging from a side road, once you've checked the pavements, you always look first towards where the traffic danger, if any, is most immediately likely. Imagine it could come from a moped whizzing along next to the gutter...One quick look, however, is not enough. You should look long enough, and at least twice in both directions, to be sure nothing can have remained hidden from you. Remember the human eye has a blind spot: and door pillars and dirty windows add more: and see fig. 15 again!

Two Faults Which Could Count Against You On Test

First, do not "swing out" as shown in fig. 16. Beginners often move forward *too quickly* – especially when there has been no need to stop – but steer *too slowly,* and a very wide turn results.

The second fault is mounting or banging the kerb. I show the problem in fig. 17, with a car entering a side road, because a biff then is often harder due to greater speed. Any severe clout can damage the tyre and pass undetected for thousands of miles – before causing a burst and, perhaps, a serious accident. Mounting the kerb is made worse if it includes a pedestrian's foot!

Your rear wheels should go smoothly round the corner, at about 2-3 tyre widths out from the kerb, as shown in fig. 14. Notice that a kerb is always rounded, making it possible to do a perfect left turn.

Turning Left Leaving A Major Road (Into A Side Road)

Countless learners make wide turns into side roads, with the car running out dangerously into the oncoming lane of the minor road as they enter it. The problem is very similar to that depicted in fig. 16. The cause is identical. They arrive *too fast* to handle the swift steering (and later straightening up) which is required. If it ever happens to you, then, in future, slow down much more, before you reach such a turn.

On a tight left hander you may even need almost to stop before your bonnet enters the turning. To prevent stalling, pop the clutch pedal down and "re-capture" a clutch slipping position just as if you were amidst a smooth take-off – although you are still slightly on the move, in 2nd rather than 1st, and no handbrake is involved. That way, you can then "drive" into the new road under controlled power, instead of rolling round into it under excessive momentum. The clutch part of the technique was more fully explained on page 26.

Check your mirrors and begin your flashing indicator signal about 75 metres from the turn. Get down the gears into 2nd and always take this left turn slowly and in control, as just emphasised above. Be on the look-out for any reason which might choke off the minor road and mean you have to stop before you can enter it. (You must always give way to a pedestrian wandering across, for example.) But do not linger unnecessarily on the major road. That can be equally dangerous, because fast major-road drivers (who may not see your problem) tend to expect you will get clear swiftly. Yes, they *are* stupid! If you have had an idiot hounding your tail, slow down for your turn with a bit more time in hand. Then, if you have to stop before you can fully enter your side road, you can do so gently, hopefully giving the goon time to see his or her folly. The time for an arm turn signal, should you decide it would be a helpful addition to your flashing indicator, is during the 3rd gear stage of slowing down.

Right Turn Off A Major Road

Let us first examine how to turn right off a major road into an isolated side road, before considering the same manoeuvre at a crossroads.

Assume you are travelling at 35 m.p.h., and a right hand turn is shortly to be taken. You are driving along normally, about half a metre from the nearside kerb.

Approximately 100 metres from your intended right turn, look in your mirrors, signal your intention, and drop to 3rd gear. Then check in the mirrors again to see that anyone behind has noted your intention, and, by about 50-75 metres from the junction, take up a "crown of the road" position if it is safe to do so. This means moving out smoothly, until positioned so that your offside (right-hand) wheels are running just to the left of the centre line, as you continue gradually to slow down.

Once you have taken up your position in the crown of the road, you must maintain it while slowing down, and you must keep your indicator flashing. Do not "wander" back to the left, or allow any vehicle behind which may be "threatening" to pass, to crowd you out of your right turn position.

If, on your second check in the mirrors, you observe a car you are not sure about, you must make your decision depending on the distance it is behind, and upon how fast it is travelling. If the

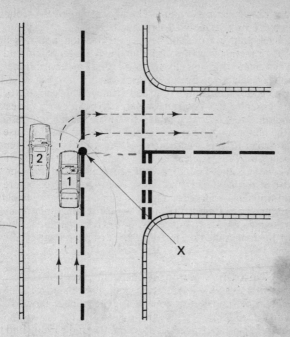

Fig. 18. Correct position should you have to wait, and the path for turning right off a major road. **Car no. 2** *passes through on the inside* if there is room, or waits behind until no. **1** has moved on into the turn.

car is travelling at about the same speed as you and is still eight or a dozen car lengths behind well after you signalled your intention, you can steer over to the crown of the road, thereby compelling that driver, when the turn is reached and if there is room, to overtake you on your left (nearside). If there is not enough room that car will have to slow down and, if necessary, stop.

If, however, it is closing up a great deal faster and the driver doesn't seem to have spotted your signal, you may have to slow

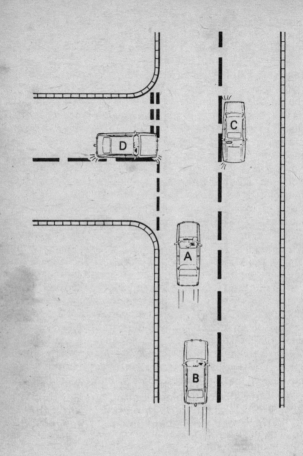

Fig. 19. Rights of way when turning right.

down and let the fellow overtake, before you take the crown of the road position. (If you are ever "menaced", despite your signal, and forced to abandon turning, take comfort that that type of driver is rare and probably does it to everyone, not just learners.)

Once there, hold the crown of the road, maintaining your

position with the offside of the bodywork moving parallel to, and just inside, the centre line of the road.

If no centre line is marked, you must visualise where it would be.

Make sure you have changed down the gears to 2nd by the time you arrive, slowly and in control, at the point where you will be making your turn. (See fig. 18.)

It is worth a pause here to consider who has precedence at the turn itself. Fig. 19 looks at this from the points of view of several drivers arriving at once. Cars A and B have the first right of way because they are not turning. They are simply going forward on their own side of the major road. C and D must wait until these have cleared. Then car C is entitled to turn to its right, safely off the major road, before car D turns out on to it.

We return to our description of turning right off a major road. You are moving slowly in the last few metres towards your turning point, in 2nd gear, ready to stop, or go on if all is clear. As just explained, the law is that you *give way* to approaching oncoming traffic, stopping if necessary. If there is nothing coming (and no problems behind), you get on and make your turn without a stop (assuming nothing blocks the road you are entering). Otherwise you stop with your front bumper level with the point marked X in fig. 18, and prepare to take 1st gear and make the turn smartly as soon as all the traffic clears. You will need the handbrake, except on a level road if you feel confident without it. Do not turn your steering in anticipation just before stopping. You do not wish to be shot forward, in the unlucky event of being hit from behind, directly into oncoming traffic!

Keep a "weather eye" on your mirrors for any two-wheelers tempted to nose up alongside on your right. They should not do it, but if they do, it is best to let them peel away first when the way clears. In your (correct) haste to get on during the first safe gap in oncoming traffic, do not forget to look where you are going to be going! Watch the neck of the turn especially, in case pedestrians might try to go across in front of you just as you are trying to enter the turn. In selecting a safe gap, always allow for such unexpected problems. Choose an opportunity in which, were you to stall for example, there still need be no accident.

After the turn, your flashing indicator, which should have been on throughout the proceedings, must be cancelled if it has not done so automatically. If you are also using an arm turn signal, give it once only, during the 3rd gear slowing down stage. It is wrong to signal, then bring the arm back, and then put it out

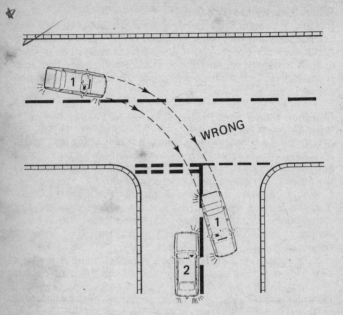

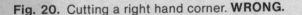

Fig. 20. Cutting a right hand corner. **WRONG.**

again as you get nearer. One continuous signal is less confusing
to others, besides possible danger to your arm and that you must
have that hand back on the wheel when you change down into
2nd, and both hands on it for the turn itself.

Your signals must be made in plenty of time. It is dangerous
and futile to drive up to within fifteen or twenty metres of the
turn, and suddenly give a right signal. If you do this, you will
"pin" other traffic behind you, unable to re-position themselves
so as to pass you on your inside, and very much to their
annoyance.

Do not worry about cars overtaking you on the inside. This is
what they are meant to do. Risk-takers regrettably sometimes
pass by very fast, through what is inevitably quite a narrow
space. They make it doubly important not to "wander" to the
left.

Where Exactly Do You Turn?

Imagine the centre line of the road you are about to turn into extended out into your road. The point round which you have to turn is the intersection of that line with the centre line of your road. **X** marks the spot in fig. 18. The correctly made right turn is one in which your car shaves round the left of this point, as shown.

Common Faults And Problems In Right Turns

You must never cut across like driver no. 1 in fig. 20. This puts at risk driver no. 2, who is also turning right, and who may not notice you about to sin until it is too late! Cutting across is a Test failure sin, whether anyone is coming out of the turning or not.

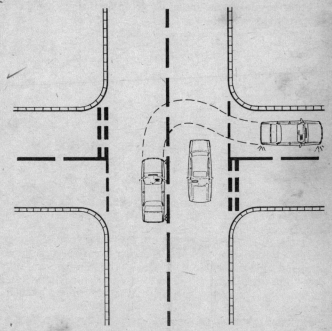

Fig. 21. Bad turn caused by creeping forward whilst the oncoming car was passing the other way. **WRONG.**

You must not creep forward as in fig. 21. Wait until you can go, following the correct line as shown in fig. 18.

Before you move across to your crown of the road position, one more factor must be taken into account. We have considered people behind, but what happens if an oncoming driver seems likely to swing across on to your half of the road as you move into place approaching your turning point? This oncoming driver might be trying to pass a slow-moving, left-turning JCB, for example, and hope to squeeze through without hitting you. Or this sort of driver might be so intent on getting round the digger that you are not seen about to turn right, at all!

Your forward planning must be a jump ahead of this inattention! Begin your moving out, but don't take up your position fully next to the line until you can see that you cannot be compromised.

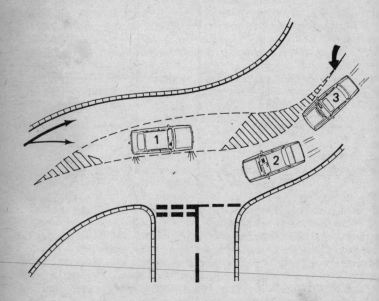

Fig. 22. Hatch road markings. Car no. **1** is correctly positioned to turn right. No. **3 MUST NOT** enter the hatched area in order to overtake no. **2**.

Hatch Road Markings

At junctions these protect right-turning vehicles from the rest of the traffic on a major road. Traffic going straight along the major road should *never* enter the hatched area. If you *are* turning right, you go into the reserve area inside the hatched part to take up your shielded right turn position. See driver no. 1 in fig. 22.

Many drivers are unaware that it is allowable, when you are turning right, to drive on to the hatching in the course of taking up the right turn position, provided the outer edge lines of the hatching have breaks as in fig. 22. This refinement helps following-drivers who are going straight on, to filter through to your left. However, it is best to wait 'til after your Test before going across the hatching itself, lest your examiner might judge you a little too clever.

These markings save many lives at turnings off major roads where there are extra hazards, such as when the junction is near a bend or brow of a hill, and where traffic overtaking foolishly might not notice a right turner having to wait in the middle. It follows that you should never overtake through a hatched area.

Sometimes hatch markings are enclosed by solid continuous white lines. This type separate opposing traffic streams at especially dangerous places such as along switch-back, up-and-down hills. Treat these hatched areas as if they were "puffed-out" double white lines. Do not drive on the hatching under any circumstances. See also Question 21 on page 154.

Turning Right Off Major Roads At Crossroads

Suppose now, that you are intending to turn right *off the major road* at a crossroads, and that a car coming the other way also intends to turn right.

All the care with your mirrors, signalling and taking a crown of the road position are the same as for the right turn above. With regard to that other car, the Highway Code lays down a basic rule that you pass *behind* each other. See fig. 23.

The expectation which stems from that rule is important. It means that, whether or not either of you may need to stop at any stage, you can each reasonably anticipate that the other will follow the strictly correct line.

(Note: the basic principle shown in fig. 23 is applied in exactly the same way turning off dual carriageways. Drivers should pass each other offside to offside, within the confines of the safe

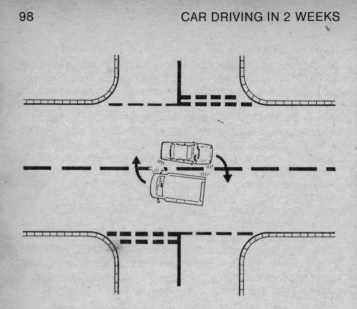

Fig. 23. CORRECT way for two drivers to turn right at crossroads. They pass behind each other, offside-to-offside.

"refuge" area (or gap) provided in the central reservation. If you have to wait before you can cross the other half of the dual carriageway, always do so in the left hand, or farther away, half of the gap insofar as is possible.)

Fig. 24 portrays a typical, but more complicated, situation. If there are a number of vehicles all wanting to turn right at the same junction, it is usual, and good driving manners, for one of the drivers to give way in order to let the opposing traffic across. Thoughtful, courteous driving will please your examiner and it will develop within you a happy motoring personality that will help reduce accidents.

The reason to go behind and not in front of each other, as a basic precept for crossroads right turns, is brought out by fig. 25. Neither driver, if you pass in front, can see properly behind the other. The restricted vision vastly increases your exposure to danger from whomsoever may try to zoom through from behind your opposite number – some motorcyclists being prime

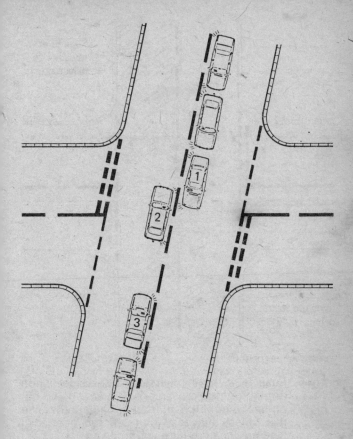

Fig. 24. A congested crossroads. Car no. 3 should wait at least until car no. **1** has been able to cross in front of it. It would be considerate to let the other two behind no. **1**, go as well, but unless no. **1** can move, nos. **1** and **2** will never be able to turn, and the whole junction will get gummed up. No. **1** must look out for traffic passing through inside on no. **3**'s left and Give Way to it, as must all who may be given the chance to follow no. **1**.

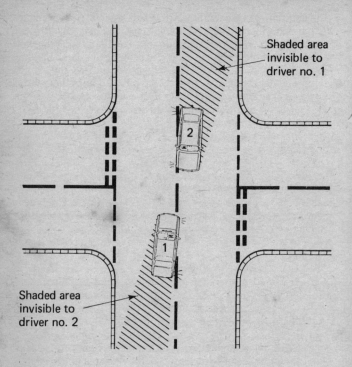

Shaded area
invisible to
driver no. 1

Shaded area
invisible to
driver no. 2

Fig. 25. Passing in front (nearside-to-nearside) when
turning right at crossroads. Drivers should not
attempt a right turn in front of one another like
this, unless space is very restricted, or special
lane markings require you to do so.

certifiable cases for so testing their luck.

All the above being said, however, sometimes, because of
restricted space at a junction, vehicles do customarily pass in
front of each other when turning right. Often you find yourself
forced to make your turn the "wrong" way by the positioning of
the driver opposite. Provided you showed extra care, you would
be unlikely to fail your Test for it. But I advise against making
yourself the instigator unless it is clearly absurd to do
otherwise.

In addition, at a great many crossroads, special road markings are painted which "channel" you into passing in front and leave you no choice. These markings are put in where the authorities recognise that the junction is going to be bunged up half the time unless drivers *do* pass in front. Many are at traffic lights. If you are turning right, position where the arrows and lines on the road show you. These helpful markings in no way remove the need for extra care which I have already stressed. *Nor does the trend towards official blessing of such passing in front, in any way alter the natural expectation of passing behind being the fundamental rule which you must always remember.*

Turning Right To Join A Major Road

Much of what you have learned so far about turning left out of a side road and turning right *off* a major road, applies. Looking in the mirrors, signalling, getting into a crown of the road position, changing down to 2nd gear if there is a give-way line so as to be ready to go should you have the opportunity, and so on, are all the same.

But there is plenty more to know:

1. As stated earlier, the **rule of the road** is that anyone turning right off the major road and into your road is entitled to go first. See fig. 19. The danger is of one of them cutting your nose off before you reach the line. See fig. 20.

2. Be ready at a crossroads for anyone opposite who is waiting to come straight across, or to make a right turn, to start out at the same instant you do. If such a driver is going straight across, it is his or her right of way. You will have to turn behind that vehicle after it has gone unless the driver clearly waits so that you can go first.

If it is turning right, you have to take into account whether you will be able to pass behind each other as per the basic rule, or if it will be more appropriate to pass in front as just discussed. You have to anticipate what the driver opposite is likely to want to do. Sometimes that wish will be clear from the angle he or she has positioned the vehicle in readiness; sometimes the road layout will preclude doubt. But unless you are certain, make *no* assumptions. Be guided not by some unofficial but cheery wave, or an incorrect and potentially ambiguous headlight flash which may be given; judge by actions. (To act on such an improper signal is at your own risk. The Highway Code directs you not to give them.) Think, before moving out, whether there is the slightest danger of the two of you getting tied up, stuck in the middle. Never risk moving if the chance of a mix up could result in major road traffic finding they had to stop unexpectedly.

If a driver opposite is turning left he or she can usually get away before you can make your right turn anyway. From a strictly technical viewpoint though, it could be argued that, once you reach into the other side of the road as you turn right into it, then if that waiting vehicle has still yet to move, it should give way to you. This is because, being already on the major road, you have right of way. But suppose that driver does not see you move forward? Why risk argument? Watch, and be ready to wait. Allow extra time just in case.

3. If the end of your side road is narrow, a full crown of the road position may be silly. Leave room for incoming traffic to get round, even big lorries.

4. When you make your right turn into the major road, having satisfied yourself it is safe and clear in both directions, it is important that your final look, made as you begin to move forward, is covering the direction having the shortest length of vision. Thus, if to the left there is a blind bend in the major road nearby to your junction, but you can see for miles to your right, your last look must be to the left. Then, if someone hurtles round that corner just as you commit yourself to go, you at least have a fighting chance to stop half-way out.

Dual Carriageways

Nasty accidents are occasionally caused in fog or on very dark nights, through the failure of a driver to observe that the road he is turning on to is a dual carriageway. Having started down the wrong half of the dual road for his direction, he may travel some distance before discovering that he is not only going the wrong way, he is also in the fast lane! Observe some typical road signs denoting where you join duals. Memorise them carefully so you can spot such a layout even in the murkiest shadows, and prevent this ever happening to you.

Mirrors, signalling, positioning and looking drill all need just as much attention when you join (or cross) a dual. And don't imagine you can approach carefree, looking only to your right; a pedestrian may well be walking across from your left...

Turning left on to a dual, go into the left hand lane as per normal lane discipline. If you were not aware you should be doing this, check through your Highway Code and see Chapter 11, page 129 of this book.

Make sure, when you **turn right** on to a dual carriageway, that you are going to be able to wait within the "safe refuge" created by the central reservation, if you need to. If there is any danger your boot could be left sticking out in the fast lane of the first half of the dual carriageway, or that your bonnet might project into the fast lane of the second half, you must wait until you have safe gaps both ways simultaneously, so that you can complete your turn in one go. Be extra careful where other vehicles are already waiting in the reservation, or if it is a very thin strip, not wide enough to contain the length of your car.

Overhanging the fast lane of a dual carriageway causes deadly accidents. Maniac speedsters, who will not slow down, never expect it, and so the side-on killer crash happens. Be prepared for others to *put themselves at risk*, but never risk it yourself.

Whenever you do have to stop within the protection of the central reservation in the course of turning right on to a dual, do so on the left side of the safe refuge, in case someone coming from your left (along the second half of the dual) also wishes to turn right. Usually, unless commonsense or *road markings* dictate otherwise, you must give way to such a driver because, theoretically, you are still on the less important road. In any case, if that driver waits for you, it is likely his or her car will mask your view of more fast traffic coming along from behind it. This other vehicle turns first, going round in front of you. (It may, of course, have to stop beside you on your right, in its half of the refuge, to wait for a clear gap in the dual carriageway traffic now passing immediately behind you.)

Whether you have had to stop in the refuge or not, you should move directly to the nearside lane as you accelerate on to the second half of the dual carriageway.

Like so many principles that bred confidence in the days of slower, lighter traffic, when you could expect people to keep to them, this one must be applied with circumspection nowadays. People break speed limits along duals. Although you may have set off with "ample" time to reach the nearside lane comfortably (where you belong unless you already need to overtake something slow like a milk float) suppose someone zooms into sight just as you are under way?

Depending how fast the vehicle is coming, and in which lane, you have to make a snap decision. Sometimes the other driver will swap lanes the instant he or she sees you, affecting your choice of action, but not always. (There may be more than one vehicle, and in different lanes, within seconds.) Although the situation may be no fault of yours, you must rapidly choose the least risky thing to do. Either:

1. Stop in your tracks so that whoever is concerned has to switch to the left lane; then go on once he, she, or they have passed, or:

2. Go as planned, accelerating like billy-ho, now forcing whoever may have suddenly appeared, to overtake you on the outside, or slow up if they cannot, or:

3. Subject to no-one just to your right trying to beat you to it (they do!), switch decisively to the right lane and go on as fast as you can accelerate. Let the speedy new arrival(s) pass you on the inside, before you move across to the nearside lane.

In theory, they certainly ought not to pass inside, but in reality, they do. Perhaps, to be fair, they are encouraged by growing numbers who, when making these turns, set off as in **3** whenever an outside lane is empty, as a matter of course – without even waiting for the nearside one to clear.

What they do may help traffic-flow at peak times but it is of doubtful legality, and it is best left to experienced drivers. As an "L", stick to the fundamental rules unless surprised into a different choice as above.

When **going straight across at a junction with a dual carriageway**, apply exactly the same care with regard to using the protection of the central reservation, and stick to the basic rules (see page 80), but be ready for others who will break them.

One-Way Streets

Most of what I have said about left and right turns has its application just the same in a one-way street. Oddities to look out for are:

1. If you are in a right hand lane flowing past a turning on your right, people about to emerge from it are often looking the other way, as they – quite wrongly – let their bonnet encroach into your one-way street. Always travel a sensible distance out from the kerb, and be ready to slow, stop, or otherwise avoid someone as careless as that. If you see one looking the other way first (unaware of your one-way street's status), a toot may wake the individual up, but never depend on that doing so in time.

2. If you are turning right at the end of a one-way street out of it, you don't use the crown of the road position; you get all the way over into the right hand lane. That seems like common-sense. The oddity is that other people – especially in a quiet one-way street – will not necessarily be expecting you to do it. Take care they cannot mistake what you are going to do.

3. You may overtake in either lane. If you are travelling in the right hand lane, then having people pass you on the left can come as a surprise, rather like having them overtake you on the inside on an ordinary road other than at a time when they are entitled to do so. The surprise element can be disturbing until you are used to it, watching your mirrors for it, and accustomed to travelling in a right hand lane instead of keeping left as per the normal rule of the road.

Well before the end of a one-way street choose the lane you are going to want, and move to it in good time, remembering all the lane-changing techniques of page 65. Don't waste an opportunity if one comes up early. Make the change then. It could save an unnecessary hold-up later, for other people too. On the other hand, if you can't change to the lane you want just yet, it may not matter on a long one-way. Don't hold everyone up if your turn is yet some way distant and you could leave the change until further along.

10

TRAFFIC LIGHTS AND ROUNDABOUTS

Always approach traffic lights with caution. Even when your direction will be straight ahead, unless you have seen them change to green within the last few moments, approach in 3rd gear at a maximum speed of about 30 m.p.h. If green has just come on, it may be reasonable to continue straight through without dropping as low as 30 m.p.h. (unless that is the speed limit anyway!) but 35-40 m.p.h. should be tops in any built-up area and I would hesitate to suggest more, even on open road dual carriageway lights. You have got to be in control for an unexpectedly quick change back to amber, then red, or for some clown crossing against red.

When the traffic light does change from green to amber as you approach, you have to make an instant decision about whether you can stop in the distance you have available, or whether to go through before red appears. You must stop unless trying to do so is likely to cause an accident.

Otherwise, carry on through the junction, but remember that if a crossing car is quick off the mark, any crash would be deemed mainly your fault. Hence, deliberately going on when you know red is certain to come on by the time you reach the lights, or if it has appeared, is highly dangerous. Police prosecute for such driving.

At traffic lights, mirrors-work, choosing the correct lane, signalling if turning, and gear changing – all on the approach – and proper use of the handbrake, should have all been absorbed from what you have read so far. The only thing to add here is that you may need to change lane even for going straight on. Select the most suitable lane long in advance. (Chapter 7 advises how, and warns that you cannot barge across lanes at the last minute.) Any free lane not baulked by, or specified with road markings solely for, turning traffic can be used. Normally stick to the one you are in unless turners are about to block it. The Highway Code commands that you do not switch to another lane merely to beat others.

When you are at the front of a queue stopped at red, wait, before taking 1st gear as part of your Smooth Take-Off, until the light changes to red and amber. However, if pedestrians are still walking across, do not take gear or, still less, bring the clutch up to the "rarin' to go" position, before they are clear – even if green comes on before that. It is safer not to. Otherwise you can complete the routine up to Step 6 (page 23), ready to go at green.

Do not rush to dart away as soon as the amber comes on with the red. It is against the law. There is still danger if another driver is yet moving through (or shooting through on the amber), from the left or right, and especially in fog. You would fail your Test. Wait for green. Even then, look out for anyone jumping the red. Last thing before moving away, double-check for pedestrians, and be on the look-out for cyclists or motor-bikers who may have crept quietly up beside you.

Traffic Lights At Roadworks
Traffic around roadworks is often controlled by a set of temporary lights. Remember, when stopping at one of these, that you must allow enough room for the largest of oncoming traffic to pass through. An articulated lorry, not yet in sight when you stop, may well turn up! (See fig. 26.) The same applies where,

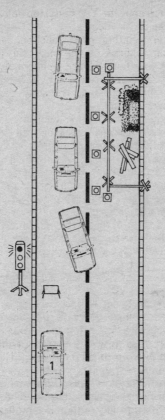

Fig. 26. Traffic lights at roadworks. Car no. **1** stops well
back and well left, to allow adequate clearance
for oncoming traffic.

instead of traffic lights, there is someone on control, with a big
red (stop) or green (go) lollipop disc. These signals must be
obeyed. Keep an eye on your mirrors so that when you move out
to get round the obstruction, you will not knock some foolhardy
two-wheelster right off.

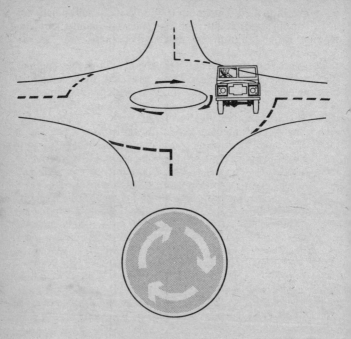

Fig. 27. "Mini" roundabout sign. The great danger at so small a roundabout is in not expecting an oncoming driver to turn right – across your bows; *that driver has right of way.* The oncoming driver here shows no signal; when you see one of the same ilk, remain suspicious until his or her front wheel direction confirms he won't swing across.

Roundabouts

There are three basic types of roundabout:

1. Enormous roundabouts (not always round) where major "through routes" intersect.

2. Ordinary "round" ones which are common where country routes meet.

3. "Mini" roundabouts. These are identified by a special sign

as shown in fig. 27. They help traffic-flow at small junctions. They vary in size from little more than a white painted circular pimple, to a "built-up" roundabout, perhaps two metres across.

There are also "roundabouts" which are so large they become miniature one-way systems. These are easy to negotiate in practice because there is more time for lane changes, but strict lane discipline has to rule.

Nearly all roundabouts have a degree of "bottle-neck" narrowing of the approach roads, or some bending of them instead, in order to slow the traffic coming in.

Whatever the type of roundabout, the correct way to drive is the same. Unless there is only one lane into the roundabout, decide which lane you will need well ahead; if you need to move lane do so early, using your mirrors and giving a brief flashing indicator signal for this change, if necessary. At the point of entry, whatever may have happened in between, always remember to double-check your mirrors last thing; glancing over your shoulder(s) may also be essential too, if you are to spot motorcycles, etc., trying to duck and weave past you.

When you reach the roundabout there should be a single-line broken "give-way" marking to define the end of your entry road. Sometimes the line may be faded or missing, but the basic rule is always the same: *Give way to all traffic from your right which is already on the roundabout.* And give way to pedestrians who, I promise you, will try to wander across the neck of your entry road just while you are looking the other way...

However, if the way is clear, go on without stopping. If you stop unnecessarily, you may hold up traffic following you, and you will possibly "cause" (see page 83) a bump from behind. (Depending where you are heading, it may be appropriate, if safe, to "flow" on to an empty roundabout lane even though another one is currently full, but I will return to the subject of which lane to use shortly.)

Once on the roundabout, you have right of way over cars entering from other roads. They ought to give way to you. However, watch carefully; many try to squeeze in front.

At a few roundabouts, exceptions to the basic rule of who gives way, are made to allow for dominant traffic-flows. Give-way lines, painted on a roundabout lane itself, instead force anyone on the way round, to give way to traffic flowing in at a particular entry point. Look out for these so you are not taken by surprise.

Lane Discipline On Roundabouts

Many roundabouts have two or more lanes all the way round. Whether these are marked or not, think in lanes. That helps *you* to avoid straying from the lane you are in, without thought for the needs and rights of others using the roundabout. Nevertheless, you are best advised to expect other drivers to fail in this regard. You do not have the right to change roundabout lanes with airy-fairy disregard to other traffic. The "who goes first" of lane changing given on page 66 has to apply, with special emphasis on giving way to anyone on your right. Note that, when you want to move directly to the innermost roundabout lane next to the middle island, a number of lane changes may be part of getting across to it, each requiring you to give way. You must not cut in front of anyone else. Some more principles must be understood when you come to leave that innermost lane. They are explained further on. Be particularly careful about those on two wheels. One of their favourite habits is to whizz around the outside edge of a roundabout, oblivious to anyone else. Develop a sweeping eye specially for them.

Turning Left At Roundabouts

Approach in the left lane. You should signal left with your flashing indicator, give way to traffic on the roundabout if necessary, and then make your left turn, keeping an eye on your mirrors and/or over your shoulder, for risk-taking two-wheelers trying to squeeze through on your nearside as you turn. They will often have a go when you have had to stop to give way to someone. It is after that that it is so important to double-check. They are encouraged when you are positioned badly – more than 2-3 tyre widths out from the kerbside. Never overtake a cyclist just as you reach the roundabout; let the two-wheeler go ahead. Then, if that person goes on round the roundabout despite all prior impressions, you won't crush the bike and its rider.

If there are two or more lanes in the road you are turning in to (e.g. a dual carriageway), you should normally go in to the left hand lane. Many drivers move directly to an outside lane to overtake, but leave such driving to faster drivers with long experience.

Going Straight Ahead (or nearly so) at Roundabouts

You can approach in any convenient lane. Give no turn signals on the approach. (You only signal for your exit.)

If you approach in a left hand lane, which is the usual thing to do unless that one is blocked, you go round in the outside lane furthest from the centre of the roundabout (giving way to your right as and if required). As you pass the first half of the exit turning *before* the one you are going to take, you begin your left flashing indicator; check behind (just as above for turning left), and leave the roundabout, again, entering your exit road in its left lane if there is more than one.

If you approach in the right hand lane of two, you then go round in the right hand lane (the lane nearest the middle island of the roundabout), after giving way to any traffic already on the roundabout.

Preparing to leave the roundabout, give your left flashing indicator several seconds earlier than above, so that roundabout outside lane traffic (to your left and perhaps further behind you) has plenty of warning of what you are going to do. You are going to have to cross their lane to reach your exit road. Watch for their reactions. Remember that, although the Highway Code asks them to **"look out for and show consideration to other vehicles crossing in front...especially...to leave by the next exit"**, you cannot cut ahead of them.

If there is no-one to your left (or "threatening" to move up there from a little behind, which, in addition to your mirrors, a quick glance over your left shoulder will confirm), and no-one is trying to muscle straight in from the exit road immediately prior to yours, you will be able to move directly across and away into the left lane of your exit road.

Be especially wary of those drivers last mentioned, who, sweeping on to the roundabout from the exit *before* the one you are aiming for, may not realise, in their indecent haste, that you are about to leave the roundabout and are not going on round. That someone like that should give way to you is true, but you must learn to expect rule-breakers.

Suppose, on the other hand, that there *is* a driver to your left, moving round the roundabout alongside you, or there is one who looks as if he or she is about to move up beside you from a fraction further back. Keeping an eagle eye on any traffic still in front of you – *because it may, and often does, unexpectedly stop* – you watch for the reaction of the driver alongside to your early signal.

By custom, if that driver slows for you, you can go on through. Otherwise, let him or her go first. Others behind shouldn't, but may attempt to go through, and you will have to wait for them.

You may even need to stop. However, such a stop should be avoided if possible, because people behind rarely expect it and may bump you.

Watch out! Such a driver alongside or coming up on your left, may well cut straight across your bows to go on round the roundabout. He or she is not necessarily making for the same exit as you!

However, if you have established *for certain* that a driver alongside *is* aiming for the same exit as you (which you do by watching for his or her positioning, speed, and signal if you can see it), there is sometimes an alternative choice. Instead of aiming for the left lane of your exit road, you may be able to enter the exit road together, still alongside each other, if there are two lanes available. This is a more skilled, though perfectly safe, manoeuvre. However, it requires a high degree of awareness of all the traffic around you and is therefore best left until you have seen it carried out properly by more experienced drivers. When safely in the exit road, unless you intend to overtake other traffic, move back to the left lane as soon as you can. Watch the mirrors first because people often – wrongly – try to pass up the inside.

Where there are three (or more) lanes round a roundabout and you are going straight ahead, you can approach in any convenient lane. However, you are expected to use the most suited lane clear at the time, so, depending on traffic congestion, you should normally favour the left or middle lanes. Whatever lane chosen for your approach to the roundabout, if you later need to swap lanes on the roundabout itself, or decide to do so, make such a transfer with care. Keep to all the rules described so far, and continually monitor what is behind or alongside. Look out especially for those on two wheels, who are so vulnerable.

Turning Right At Roundabouts
Your approach should be in the right hand lane, if there is more than one, signalling as usual before moving to this lane. Head directly for the innermost lane on the roundabout, next to the middle island, but give way to others already coming round – as you are required to do by the basic rule. Keep your right flashing indicator on all the time, including whilst you go round, right up to the point when you need to change it to the left one as you prepare to move off the roundabout. Transfer across to your exit road using exactly the same principles and care already described above.

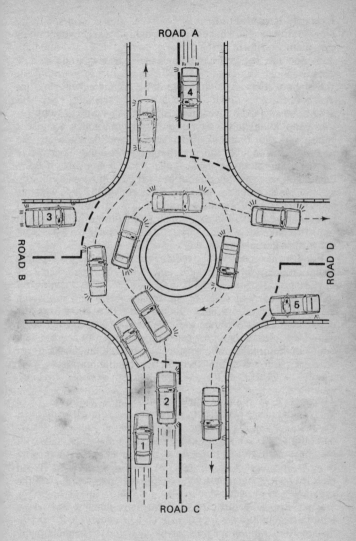

Fig. 28. A busy urban roundabout showing the intended route of each car.

Example Roundabouts
Now look at fig. 28, a busy roundabout in a town. In your mind's eye, picture yourself as the driver of cars no. 1, 2, 3, 4 and 5, in turn. See whether you understand the right way to do it, now described.

Since no. 2 has signalled a right turn, no. 1 can begin to filter to its left, and pass 2 on the nearside as and when safe. They both need to be keeping a "weather eye" to make sure 3 is stopping. Car 3 should anyway wait a little back from the line because it can see 1 and 2 are likely to be able to "flow" on to the roundabout without a stop, and that therefore it will have to give way to them. Stopping short, "tells" them 3 is aware. If no. 4 intends leaving the roundabout at road B, it must wait initially for no. 2 as it comes round. Then 4 can go, while no. 5, who has been a bit slow off the mark, waits. Car 5 will have to do that unless, as here, there is room to slip left without frightening 4. Note that 5 could have gone earlier whilst 2 blocked 4's passage, but it missed that opportunity.

Fig. 29 shows an "odd" roundabout. Car no. 1 gives a right signal from A, a left one from B, and makes for its exit. Car 2, as it is going straight on, normally gives no signal. Car 3 gives a left signal from early on as he or she approaches. Car 2, if turning left at the second entrance, should only signal left from the centre of the first entrance to the left of the diagram. Driver 2 must be on the look-out for car 4 pushing its way aggressively out from that first entrance just as 2 is trying to ease over to the nearside. Car 4 ought to know better, but Saints are in short supply!

Timing – And Which Gear To Use At Roundabouts
Which gear to use depends on your speed, which will be dictated by the size and shape of the roundabout and by traffic conditions. At a huge multiple-intersection roundabout, you may have no need to change down below 3rd gear if there is no other traffic to slow you down. At a busy roundabout in the middle of a town, you may have to stop half-way round and then start again in 1st gear.

If you are the leading car, always change down to 3rd during your initial approach. Get your speed down nearer to 20 m.p.h. than to 30 m.p.h. If your way will be clear and the roundabout is suitably large to keep going at 20 m.p.h. +, stay in 3rd. If it is obvious a stop will be unavoidable, you can pull up in 3rd; there is no need to bother with 2nd. Then you can use your handbrake,

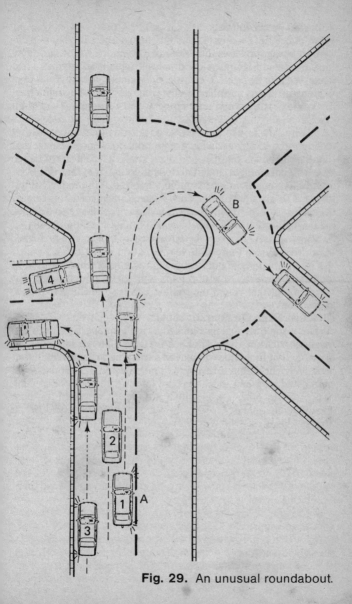

Fig. 29. An unusual roundabout.

followed by the full Smooth Take-Off routine with 1st gear, as soon as it's safe to go.

Otherwise, however, always drop to 2nd a good 50 metres out. Provided you now slow down sufficiently in advance, 2nd gear, with its zippy acceleration, will enable you safely to take advantage of any suitable gap that may appear, and which then makes it possible for you to slip on to the roundabout without a stop.

Always try to use a decent gap, but don't get carried away trying to be too clever with your roundabout entry timing; and don't try to be too smart accelerating ahead in an effort to change lanes during going round. There's rarely much to be lost by the alternative of slowing or stopping, and then slipping in behind those who are really there first. Indeed, misplaced enthusiasm for getting in front often results in a shunt. The driver concerned, instead of *looking where he or she is going,* is too busy looking towards what it is hoped will become a gap to merge in to. Either that driver doesn't pay sufficient attention to the vehicle which he or she is immediately following, who then decides to stop despite a perfectly splendid gap, or he or she fails to see that everyone further round the roundabout is screeching to a halt.

Blocked Exits On Roundabouts
When your own exit is blocked, with a queue back into the roundabout, don't be a blockhead. There is no need to block off some entry point which you need to pass in order to reach your exit. Why sit across an entry/exit point you don't happen to be interested in, when those you are holding up could be making their way to other exists which are clear? Stop and let them across your queue. Use the box junction concept and be an unblockhead!

11

OVERTAKING

Whilst you are on the wrong side of an ordinary two-way road such as I deal with first, you are taking many additional risks. If you have, or cause, any accident out there, you will almost certainly be held entirely to blame. Therefore, *before* moving to overtake, you must be sure of everyone's safety.

Part of this must include checking intelligently in your mirrors – details on that shortly. You must begin your right flashing indicator signal *before* pulling out. When you go, keep it flashing up to the stage you begin moving back in after the overtake. Then cancel it. Although you have taken care no-one will be endangered by your overtake, the signal is still essential; it may warn someone you failed to notice; it confirms what you are doing, both to everyone else around, and to anyone arriving on the scene whilst you are in progress. A left flashing indicator as you start to move in is hardly ever necessary. The way you are pointing the car should itself tell people what you are doing. I would only add the signal, so as to confirm what was happening, if I had to move back in more sharply than expected.

When Not To Overtake
The Highway Code specifies places which you should not overtake at (or when approaching); *learn them by heart*.

It also wisely says "IF IN DOUBT – DO NOT OVERTAKE".

The general rule is that you must not overtake unless you are certain that the road is clear, and that there *will be a gap for you in your stream* – into which you can return without hindrance.

At no stage should an oncoming driver have to slow down or brake because of you. For someone to have to brake hard could be dangerous. A situation where someone coming was forced to swerve out of your way would be even more so.

Nevertheless, if someone is overtaking *towards you,* ease off your accelerator until you can see that they will be back on their own side well before you arrive. It helps no-one if you bash on and risk lives all round.

How To Overtake
To overtake safely, you should be accelerating to at least 15-20 m.p.h. faster than the vehicle you are passing. Sometimes, with care, you can put on most of this higher speed before you even move out; a more advanced driver will use an acquired sense of timing to do this instinctively, both so that he or she can make 100% safe use of a shorter gap in oncoming traffic than a less experienced driver might do, and so that the least possible time will be spent exposed to danger, on the wrong side of the road.

The more quickly you can complete your overtake, the better – provided there is *no likelihood* of the driver you are passing pulling out on you (for example to get past a cyclist who has been hidden from your view). Beware, however, of too large a difference between your speeds just as you begin to pass. Always ask yourself: "If that vehicle *does* pull out just as I'm coming up, how quickly can I react and pull in behind?"

Prior to overtaking, move up reasonably close behind the vehicle you want to pass. But remain far enough back to see clearly past without endangering yourself, either by then finding you need to get too far out in the road in order to see, or by getting so close you will be in trouble if the driver of that vehicle slams his or her brakes on.

The best "ready" viewing position is usually **much farther back than you expect,** particularly when you are behind a large lorry or a 'bus! Being further back allows, through curves in the road, etc., opportunities to spy ahead which are denied if you are too close.

You remain "ready" until, either, (a) you can see that you can pass and have time to return to your side safely – and so you do, or, (b) you can see it won't be safe, and so you drop back again temporarily. Never stay close, as if on the point of passing, when you know that you can't go anyway at the moment. Cancel your signal meantime.

Apart from in a queue, at all times maintain a substantial safe gap between yourself and whatever is in front of you. It is selfish, as well as dangerous, to drive close when you do not intend to overtake. Being able to stop if that driver does, is fundamental.

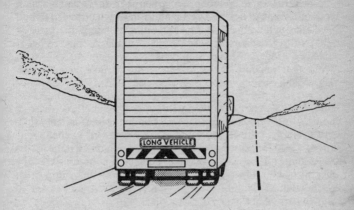

Fig. 30. You are clear to overtake the lorry.

Additionally, the Highway Code makes it clear that gaps need to be seen to be available by people who want to overtake – who may wish to pull in in front of you. The Code also insists that you *slow down,* if it is necessary, in order to let someone passing you pull in safely. When someone does fill the gap you have been leaving, you must drop back further and create a fresh one.

Look at fig. 30. You are driving in the "ready" position behind a lorry, having previously checked your mirrors over enough distance to be sure that no-one is hoping to pass you; the road ahead is clear and straight and you have started your right flashing indicator signal. None of the Code-specified reasons against overtaking are in evidence. You are clear to overtake. You double-check your mirrors and there are still no worries there.

With no doubt whatever, go, quickly. Do not linger once you have decided. Otherwise cancel your signal and drop back, as already explained, until another opportunity to move up "ready" arises.

Leave a door's width, and a bit more for good measure, between you and the vehicle you are passing.

In the "ready" position it is essential to be in the right gear for maximum acceleration. You want to minimise the length of time that you go out on to the wrong side of the road, and the right gear makes sure that you can do so. Below about 15 m.p.h. use

2nd gear; reckon to change up *after* you pass. In the same way, if your initial speed lies between 20 and 50 m.p.h., use 3rd to add speed throughout the pass. Do not normally change up to 4th (or 5th) until you are safely back on your own side. A "missed" gear change during overtaking may cause an accident. In a car with five gears, remember 4th will have much more acceleration power than 5th.

Bad Advice About "Cutting In"
Learners are often told to wait, before moving back in, until they can see in their mirrors, at least the front wing of the vehicle they have passed. This crazy, amateur, advice, is handed out with the air of authority of a police regulation, as if cutting in was the biggest of all motoring sins. In fact your only duty, in normal circumstances, is not to cause the driver concerned to have to slow down or brake.

I'm not suggesting you should ever cut in without reason. However, following that mirrors' method keeps you in danger, on the wrong side, far too long. In those extra seconds you could be killed. Dramatic language perhaps, but it is just at such times that things go wrong. A nutcase racing motorcyclist, for example, may appear from round the next bend at 120 m.p.h., that rider presuming that his or her side, will be clear. I can assure you there will be many times when you bless the fact you moved in promptly.

If your speed is much faster than that of the person you are overtaking, then because you are pulling ahead so rapidly, you can move in amazingly soon without that driver having to slow down. A quick glance over your shoulder proves this, and helps you judge it. When your speed is not much above that of whoever you are passing, you have to leave it a little later; however, if you cannot muster sufficient acceleration to complete the pass swiftly – why are you doing it?

In emergency, do not be afraid to cut in quite fiercely. If faced with a choice of a head-on collision or just bumping the chap you are passing, the latter must be the safer alternative. That vehicle is going at much the same speed as you, and a bump would probably amount to little. Its driver might have seen the crisis anyway, and braked out of your way. But even a brush with someone coming the other way could turn into a major smash, with some of those involved probably being flung into the ditch, and many additional vehicles and casualties caught up in the mêlée.

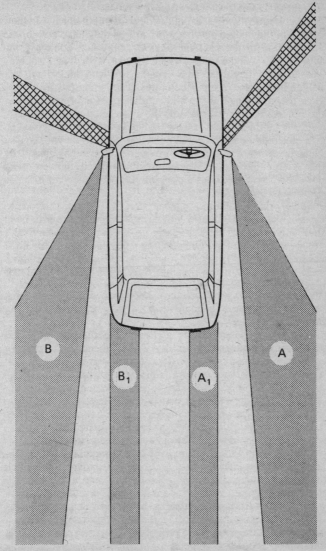

Fig. 31. Mirrors and door pillars blind spots.

Common Dangerous Overtaking Errors

Drivers frequently over-estimate the power of their cars. In their optimism they begin passing, only to find they have not got the acceleration to get past *in time*. Or, they just don't use the acceleration (via the gears), which they have got. Their troubles worsen when they try to pass a mad driver who thinks he or she will enjoy a "dice", and accelerates. They end up dangerously close to overtaking round a blind corner, or else forced to jam on the brakes, hoping to return to the space they started from.

Far from thinking of "racing" when you are being overtaken (which would be illegal), you need your wits about you; so that you can slow down and allow an overtaker who has misjudged things to get back in, or you can maintain speed (or even speed up) should you see that that person has seen the error and has decided to drop back.

Judge your acceleration power carefully. A good motto is to "pass only when you know you have 30% more power in hand than you expect to use". In early days when, even as an "L", you need to pass a slow-moving vehicle, your instructor must guide you as to whether your car has enough speed in hand. Later on, be sure to extend your experience gradually, especially when, after your Test pass, you're on your own.

A second common error is to omit that final double-check in the mirrors before overtaking. Quite often, in a line of traffic, the driver of a fast car at the rear will happen to be the earliest to be in a position to see that the road is clear. With that car's extra reserve power he or she attempts to shoot past the whole line of vehicles. If you swing out, you may cause a serious accident. The *rule of the road* is to **give way to the overtaking driver.** He or she may, seeing your intention from your signal, be a fool, but anyone who is out there first is within their rights. They are entitled to regard your signal as being of intention only.

Fig. 31 shows amazingly large areas **A** and **B** in which a car – or even a lorry – which is about to overtake, can be invisible to you during a once-only check in the mirrors. To spot every car or motorcycle, continuous mirrors checking is essential, not just a quick glance before you move out.

Even so, despite the most responsible of mirrors work, a nagging doubt sometimes creeps in at the last second as to whether anyone is hidden there. (Has a daring motorbiker swept up to pass, out from B_1, fig. 31, through A_1, for example?) At the point of moving out to overtake, therefore, the experienced driver will slide a nifty glance over his or her right shoulder – just

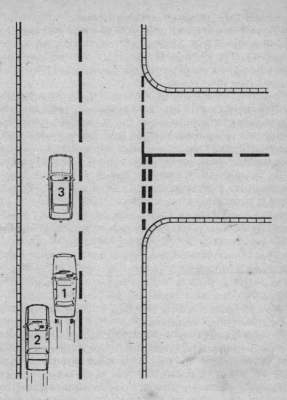

Fig. 32. A false sense of security.

enough to spot anyone "breathing" up there.

Poor mirrors use, particularly causes accidents on motorways and dual carriageways. There, a long distance rear view is essential because people can zoom up behind very fast, from "nowhere".

A third overtaking error is where you, as the overtaking driver, passing a large lorry, fail to notice that its driver has been (dangerously) tail-gating a small "old banger" just in front of it. That "banger" could rob you of your required space to get back in the traffic stream.

Your "ready" position must be far enough back from the lorry for you to avoid this trap; apart from offering better opportunities of being able to pick a safe gap for overtaking, which are very necessary, the extra space provides moments to see past immediately in front of the lorry at bends, or to look underneath it going over the brow of a hill.

A fourth overtaking error often causing accidents, happens on fairly wide roads with two lanes of traffic in each direction. As you are using the outer of these lanes to overtake, rather than the wrong side of the road, you can be lulled into a false sense of security. Suppose the outer stream is travelling a wee bit faster than traffic in the inside lane, and you – no. 1 in the outer lane as in fig. 32, along with everyone else in your lane – have been continuously overtaking those in the inner lane. Before you know it, car no. 3 in front, which you think is merely continuing with this overtaking, is, in fact, slowing down ready for turning right. By the time you realise, it may be somewhat late to draw up behind 3, and impossible to get back into the left hand lane because of 2. Admittedly, 3, in this picture, neither signalled, nor positioned well so as to make his or her intention obvious (and, maybe, the car's brakelights had failed), but that is no excuse for you; as a reader of this book you ought to have spotted you were following a wally, a long ways earlier!

Alternatively, your problems could have come to a head before you began to overtake 2. Imagine that 2 suddenly decided to swing across and turn right, just before you got alongside, and that its driver never saw you in his or her mirrors... Despite the "secure" feeling that can take hold in the sorts of conditions described, you must remember that your stream is nevertheless overtaking the inside one, and that to be actually passing one of the inner stream at, or approaching, a junction, puts you in the wrong. The Highway Code warns against *any* such overtaking.

Drivers who do so, risk spectacular, death's-door crashes. Take the overtaken driver in fig. 33, who had been slowing down to allow the car waiting in the side road to come out and turn right. That driver never expected that good deed to herald a serious smash, but two fatal errors strode in. The impatient fellow behind ignored the junction and tried to accelerate past. The driver emerging from the side road did so too quickly to stop, even though looking the right way at the right time. He or she assumed *all* the traffic from the right would stop...An even worse mistake would have been to try to cut across on the way out and round...

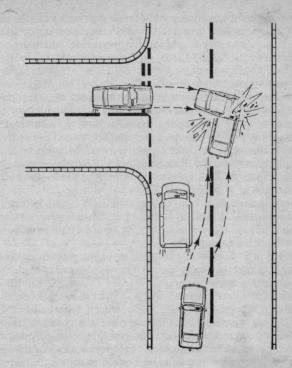

Fig. 33. Fatal errors.

A fifth principal overtaking area for misjudgments occurs on "killer" three-lane roads. These are *two-way* roads where the centre lane is for overtaking or turning right only. Lane divisions into three are not always marked; indeed, sometimes there is actually a centre line trying to denote two lanes only, but local practice and relentless heavy traffic mean that three-lane conditions are a fact of life. Traffic in either direction *will* use the centre – laned or not.

Only custom really dictates who you are going to find there in the middle. Traffic going one way has no more right to be there than that going the other way. "First come, first served" is the best way to describe what should happen, but you dare not rely on it. Once you have moved to the middle (assuming it was clear first!), approaching drivers should treat it as yours and not pull out. The trouble is, they often ignore this reasonable basis. Equally, when anyone coming the other way has started to overtake or is "established" in the middle, don't you move out!

I hope these "killer" roads will be phased out eventually in favour of dual carriageways, but in the meantime, the safest advice is never to overtake while traffic is thick and fast. The chance that a driver from the other direction will risk breaking custom, regrettably, places you at what I believe to be too high a risk. If one does pull out despite your already being in the middle, give him or her priority; get back in. Avoiding a smash is more important than arguing the toss afterwards (if you are lucky enough to be around...).

During daylight, if I am in the middle, high risk, lane, I switch on headlights, as well as my normal right flashing indicator signal, 'til I am ready to move in. (At night I would have dipped headlights on anyway.)

Move in as directly as you can after passing. On these "fast" roads, unexpected traps – like running out of petrol or a smashed windscreen – often spring!

As a rule, keep your "door's width and a bit for good measure" alongside passing-gap which I advised earlier, but realise that it is stupid to be that far from what you are passing, and only perhaps half the distance away from traffic zipping the other way. If the circumstances were that tight, you must have been trying to pass in a dangerous place. However, should you find yourself in such a predicament, *move in half your door's width*. Then you will have a half door's width gap, plus your good measure, on the "good" side, and be leaving a full door's width (and a touch more of good measure!) on the "deadly" side.

In normal conditions of ample room, therefore, always position yourself so that most of the spare gap is on the "bad" side. Keep away from danger, nearer safety.

Sometimes at long hills, double white lines divide these three-lane roads, as to two lanes uphill and one lane downhill. Look at those lines *carefully*. It is not necessarily safe to assume that you can always move, free of danger from oncoming traffic, into the outer lane in the uphill direction. Whenever the double white line nearest the single lane *is a broken one*, oncoming traffic *is* free to move out and use that lane coming *towards you*, just as if it were an ordinary middle lane of three...

The sixth dangerous overtaking factor which I will mention, is failure to notice that the gap you plan to move back in to, is shrinking. The traffic stream, further ahead than you have been looking, is stopping! I have several times risked repeating that you must always be *looking where you are going,* because of all the faults *all* learners make, forgetting this one is the most popular, and the most deadly. And the worst part of it is not looking *far enough* ahead. You must learn to match your driving to the ever-changing situation right out to the horizon on the road in front. You're not looking far enough ahead until you never miss a trick between you and the most distant point that the eye can see. If you're not getting it right, the shrinking gap will one day catch you out.

The Warning Hoot
Whenever you overtake, assume that the driver you are about to pass is unaware of it, unless you have seen that person notice you. If there is any chance the driver could inadvertently compromise the safety of your pass, give a toot, once within earshot. Then your presence should be known, but never depend on it; the driver may be deaf.

Overtaking On Dual Carriageways
When you want to move to an outer lane to pass someone, there should be fewer problems in front, but watch out! *All* lanes ahead could be piling up into an accident! *Keep the long view, way out ahead, well within your focus.*

Once you are in a middle or outer lane you may want to overtake more than one vehicle before moving in, provided you feel your continuing progress will not unnecessarily hold up faster traffic arriving behind. (You do not want to become a moving obstruction!) There is no need to continue with your right flashing indicator for this additional overtaking. Cancel it. (Its use was to show you were intending to move out – not that you are staying there! If you are now in a middle lane it could confuse those passing in an outside lane anyway.)

A priority, as you reach each of a row of vehicles you are passing, is to watch none of them pull out on you. If anyone "threatens" to at a crucial moment, or does, you have to decide whether you are still safe to go on, or you MUST brake, and let the person out. A (gentle) hoot in time may warn the driver you are there if he or she has not seen you.

What you must never do, if you are in a middle lane, is

suddenly to swing out into a lane outside yours. **Stay in lane.**

Swerving out causes many bad accidents. It is all very well to assume an outside-lane driver coming up fast will have been watching the whole developing scenario of death, and slowing up in case (as I pray you always will if you are that driver), but the terrible fact is, most do not. Be warned.

No Overtaking On The Inside

There are only four exceptions when it is right to overtake on the inside, apart from on one-way streets. In practically all other circumstances doing so is *dangerous* and contrary to the Highway Code. The exceptions are:

1. When you are correctly passing through on the left of someone who has signalled his or her intention to turn right and is slowing down. (Note that *for this purpose you must not enter a 'bus lane during its period of operation.* You must wait.)

2. When you are in a left hand lane in stop/start queueing lanes of traffic, and that inside lane is, for the time being, moving up faster than the next outer one (e.g. on a dual carriageway if an outer lane is blocked by roadworks and all lanes are down to walking pace). However, you are not supposed to chop and change lanes for temporary advantage.

3. If you are turning left shortly and an inside lane (but not a 'bus lane at reserved times) is free to take you there, while others carrying straight on may be having to slow or stop.

4. When your lane at traffic lights enjoys a lit green left filter arrow, whilst red continues to hold others.

There is, and should be, a general expectation among drivers that, apart from the above times, they will *not* have people trying to zip by inside them while they are travelling at the general traffic speed. It doesn't make any difference whether they are going along in a wide single lane, or, if they expect soon to be overtaking, in an outer lane if there happens to be more than one.

They need to know that it will be safe to move in quickly if sudden danger forces them to. Unfortunately on our overcrowded roads, an increasing number of drivers are flouting the safety rules and will not wait for you to move over (as you should directly you can) when they want to pass. They pass you on the inside, with hardly a second thought. You just have to watch out for them. Only your mirrors or a glance over the shoulder can alert you to such dare-devils – especially the two-wheeled types

– but you may not have time to worry about them too much in a life or death emergency, one which forces you left without time to stop instead.

If only every driver would consistently move to the most leftward lane available, as instructed by the Highway Code, the reason for all this rule-breaking by people wanting to pass, would be removed.

The growing menace of illegal inside overtaking makes using a left flashing indicator signal prior to moving to a lane on your left doubly important, even though you can expect most of those lawless drivers to ignore signals as well as rules.

Overtaking Cyclists

Never pass too close to cyclists. Try to give them at least a door's width, plus a little; they often "wobble". If a cyclist is already "wobbling", or looks likely to, give a gentle toot well before you overtake. Cyclists usually "wobble" more going uphill and they frequently make wide detours for manhole covers, etc. If you are going to have to move out, even a little amount, *always* signal beforehand; people behind need to know. When a cyclist is coming the other way, remember motorists trying to pass that bike may suddenly swing out quite substantially – temporarily forgetting about you!

If a cyclist ahead of you signals to turn right and pulls across to the crown of the road, give lots of extra room if/when you pass on the inside. Move in earlier than usual, if you safely can; then people behind you should spot the cyclist in such a vulnerable position, sooner than they might otherwise do.

The Highway Code instructs you, **"Do not overtake a cyclist or motorcyclist immediately before turning left..."**. Let them get on ahead of you.

12

MANOEUVRES, REVERSING, PARKING

Most learners dread the two special manoeuvres required in the Driving Test – reversing into a limited opening, and turning round in a narrow quiet road ready to go back the other way (the "three-point-turn"). Both are easy with good clutch control, and good steering in reverse which is discussed next.

Beyond the Test, ability to manoeuvre safely in tight spaces on your own is essential, for example, in a multi-storey car park.

Steering In Reverse

Have in mind to start with, the four corners of your car. Split the car in your mind, down the bonnet, down the centre between the passenger and driver's seat, and out through the rear window. You are sitting in your half of the car, and your instructor is sitting in the other half. Also draw an imaginary line down through the steering wheel from 12 o'clock to 6 o'clock.

Your mind's-eye should have no difficulty seeing which two corners of the car are in your half, and which two are in the other. The thing to remember for reversing, is that your half is controlled by the right half – your half, in fact – of the steering wheel, and the other half – your instructor's half – is controlled by the left half of the steering wheel. Although the same is equally true going forwards, this visualisation helps you remember which way the wheel must be turned when going backwards.

In reverse, if you want the rear nearside (the passenger side) to go further to that side, you begin by pulling down the left half of the steering wheel. In other words, whichever direction you wish a half of the car to go, that is the side – or half – of the

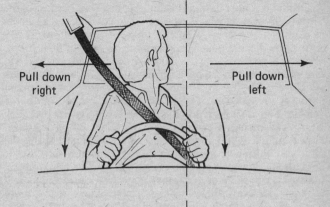

Fig. 34. Steering in reverse.

steering wheel, which you pull down. It is as simple as that. See fig. 34.

Apart from quick glances to the front and sides to see that no danger is arising, remember that when you are reversing, your *first duty* must be *looking behind!*

Always turn yourself well round in your seat and, for reversing, **look over your left shoulder.** Use the steering wheel in exactly the same way for reverse as you learned for going forwards. However, you can, if turning round far enough for long enough is a problem, modify the basic steering wheel holding position when going straight back more than a few metres. Instead of having your hands between "ten to two" and a "quarter to three", adopt a hold in which the right hand is comfortably gripping around 12 o'clock and the left maintains a loose grip about 8 o'clock. Small amounts of steering to keep straight are then easier. But remember that you must not let this modified method degenerate into ever crossing your hands on the wheel. That spells Test failure! For the rapid turning of the wheel needed in tight manoeuvring, you must still revert to the standard wheel handling method given in Chapter 4.

What Is A Three-Point-Turn?
Do not regard this as a method of turning round in a major road. I
deal with that under the next heading but one. The purpose of the
three-point-turn is to demonstrate that you can control a vehicle
in a restricted space. A Test examiner cannot afford to risk
letting you damage other cars by trying to park in their midst.
Therefore, you are taken to a narrow street instead, and asked to
turn round between the pavements, using 1st and reverse gears
alternately. See fig. 35. If your car wheels strike the pavement
during this manoeuvre, it is obvious that you cannot control the
vehicle. You are not supposed to let the car bodywork overhang
either pavement, either, unless it is clear of pedestrians.
However, unless you do go right up to each pavement during the
turn, you will never succeed in doing the neatest turn that is
possible. If, doing the best the car's steering will allow, you still
have to take five moves rather than only three, the examiner will
be satisifed. Nevertheless, he or she is likely to be more
impressed by a neat three-point-turn, provided the street is wide
enough to allow for it. Most cars can be three-point-turned
easily in a street about 7½ metres wide; doing the turn in a street
wider than that is hardly a test!

The best way to discover how near the kerb you are with the
front or the back of the car when you are practising, is to stop
between the moves. Set the handbrake, select neutral, and get
out and look for yourself.

How To Do The Three-Point-Turn
You have pulled up at the kerbside on the left, at the examiner's
request; the handbrake is on, and you are in neutral. You have
been told that this is where you are to turn the car round between
the pavements using forward and reverse gears, when you are
ready.

As you are not expected to give signals during the three-point-
turn, you must particularly wait 'til all traffic is clear in both
directions. Thereafter, what you are doing should be obvious to
anyone coming along.

SAFETY, during the three-point-turn, is paramount. You
must keep a quick eye out in each direction during the first move
forward. Look both ways again, *before* reversing back. Watch
for anyone turning up during that reverse. And look both ways
again, before the final forward move. If traffic appears at any
stage, you should allow it to pass, by waiting for it to do so
between your moves, but do *not* wave people through. Let them

decide. If they clearly want to wait, get on with your turn. Watch out for children *all the time* especially when reversing; they can be quick to leave a pavement and try to run behind your car.

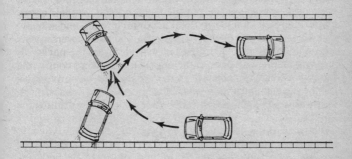

Fig. 35. Three-point-turn front wheel positions.

So, only begin when the street is clear for a long distance both ways. Starting to move very slowly, with clutch control in 1st gear, whip the steering wheel round rapidly towards the opposite pavement during the first metre, so as to complete a full wheel lock (the wheels turned as much as they can) as soon as possible. (Do not turn the steering wheel before you have begun to move the car. Even though power steering, if you have it, would conceal much of the extra effort required, doing so can strain the steering joints and is bad for the tyres.) Keep the car moving extremely slowly across the road, holding the steering wheel on that full lock.

It will be necessary to "slip the clutch" to control your speed at the snail's pace which is essential as you start off, and for the same control as you reach the opposite kerb. Snail's pace driving, explained near the end of Chapter 2, is the secret which allows you the time to make the rapid steering lock change. Remember to steal some glances both ways in case anyone comes along.

Depending on the width of the road, you may be able to release the clutch pedal fully and go a tiny bit faster, as you go across the middle. However, if it is narrow, clutch control of speed may be necessary all the time.

You must have that snail's pace control again for the last 1-2 metres as you reach the opposite kerb; so, if the clutch pedal has been fully released during the crossing over stage (which it should be if it is possible), you pop it back down as far as the "slipping" point, in good time. But this may not be enough. If the road dips in towards the pavement edge, or if you have gone faster than you should, you will need the footbrake as well, to trim speed back to a snail's pace for the final metre or so. Because during that last distance you have got to change the steering all the way back to the opposite lock, or as nearly that far as you can. Your objective is to have the steering as prepared for the reverse back as is possible.

Front wheel positions at each point of the turn are shown in fig. 35.

Because of the way the car nearly always tries to roll on into the gutter, you must always reckon to control the exact stopping position – before the wheels hit the pavement – with the footbrake, clutch pedal down by this time, to prevent stalling. Then put on the handbrake.

With skill and much practice, you will now have the steering wheel already turned and in full lock the other way, prior to your reverse to the pavement you started from. Remember (because of the strain on the parts) not to go on steering after you have stopped the car moving. If you have not quite managed full lock, you can turn the wheels the last little bit just as you start off in reverse. However, the best turns are accomplished when the steering lock change is completed just as you stop.

Check for traffic in both directions. Wait, if need be, 'til clear again. Now – looking backwards over your left shoulder – reverse slowly back. (You may need your best uphill start technique to prevent running forward into the gutter.) There is no need unduly to dawdle across the middle, but when the rear of your car is two metres or a bit less from the kerb you started from, you must be back down to snail's pace control. This will enable you to turn the steering rapidly back towards the same lock you started with, during the last metre or so, just before you stop. Be ready with the footbrake, and stop before the back of the car overhangs the kerb. Put on your handbrake again. Did you manage quick glances both ways during that reverse...?

You are now ready for a smooth take-off in 1st gear to complete your turn – other traffic permitting, as ever. If you are still not going to clear the opposite kerb, then another reverse will be necessary. Swing to the other lock for this in good time, using the same technique explained.

Sometimes, if the road is not very narrow, reversing all the way back to the first kerb is unnecessary; half or three-quarters of the way is enough before you know you can easily get clear when you move forward. If so, get back into right hand full lock that much earlier. *Never reverse further than necessary.*

On completion of your turn, drive on, unless the examiner asks you to pull up in a parked position. For the latter, see **Pulling In To Stop Next To The Kerb,** page 38.

Changing Direction On A Major Road

Suppose you have missed the turning you meant to take off a major road. You need to turn and go back the other way. No examiner would expect you to do this as part of your Test, but you may be asked a question to make sure you are aware of the correct way it should be done.

As emphasised already, a busy major road is *not* the place for a three-point-turn! Ideally, keep going 'til you can turn off left into a smaller, quieter road; then go along that 'til you reach a suitable empty side road, again, on your left, to use to back into for turning. A less ideal thing, is to use a small road to your left, directly off the major road. But at least you can sometimes spy whether it is empty when you first pass it, which is a great help.

What you do *not* do, under any circumstances, is to take a left turn and then reverse out into the major road. Nor do you cut across the major road to reverse into a side road on that side.

Having chosen the road you intend to use to reverse into, follow the routine given below for the similar reverse into a limited opening. Only back into the side road as far as necessary to enable you to take up a proper right turn position for re-emerging.

Where your major road is very wide, there may be an alternative way to turn around, known as a U-turn. See question 53, Chapter 16. My advice, because it is tricky to do, is only to attempt a U-turn at times when traffic is very light.

Reverse Into A Narrow Or Limited Opening

On Test, so that you can demonstrate skill reversing round a corner into limited space without risk to other vehicles, the examiner will choose a suitable narrow side street leading off a *minor* road. You will be asked to pull in beyond the turning.

Your examiner will give plenty of advance notice, and it will be up to you to time your pulling in signal, so that no-one might think you were simply turning into the road (see page 75). Usually, a left hand opening is chosen. If the examiner wants you to reverse round into a right hand corner (which the examiner can, especially if you take your Test in a small van from which it is harder to see out of the back), you will need to cross to the offside before you can pull up beyond the selected turning. In this case, you treat the initial stage just like turning right, taking up a crown of the road position before the final move over. Give way to oncoming traffic if necessary, and be just as careful no-one could misinterpret your signal. If you have to wait at the crown of the road, then doing so a little way past the opening ensures that it will be obvious you are not turning directly into it.

As with the three-point-turn, having reached the starting position, you are not expected to include signals during the exercise itself. However, you are here making a turn (albeit in reverse) off one road into another. I believe it is safer therefore, although you wait for other traffic at all stages, to put on the relevant flashing indicator before you begin. This extra care should please any examiner.

I begin with the reverse to the left. It is often regarded as more difficult because the width of the car is between the driver and kerb. Nonetheless, the right hand reverse has its problems and I come to them separately later. You are expected to know how to cope with either reverse.

Reversing To The "Difficult" Side
You are expected to follow the kerb round, keeping to your own side as you enter the limited opening, and reverse back 'til asked to stop reasonably close to your nearside kerb.

Let us assume your starting position is several car lengths beyond the turning, pulled in beautifully close to the kerb. Your wheels are comfortably within two tyre widths of the gutter edge, just as they should be, and your steering is aligned straight ahead.

The ideal distance out for the car to be when you come to round the corner is 3-4 tyre widths. In order to gain this gap you need to ease out *gently,* especially to begin with, as you cover the ground towards the corner; you cannot swing the steering wheel sharply, or your front left wheel simply biffs the kerb and may mount it.

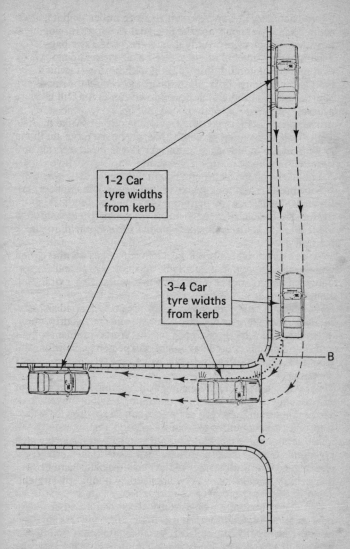

1–2 Car tyre widths from kerb

3–4 Car tyre widths from kerb

Fig. 36. Reversing into a narrow street to the "difficult" side.

As discussed, put on your left flashing indicator before you begin. When you approach the line A-B as in fig. 36, you must be moving much more slowly than you crawled as a baby! You must maintain control of your speed exactly as you want it by "slipping the clutch". If a downhill slope is causing the car to run too fast, you must hold your speed back with the footbrake instead, pushing the clutch pedal down for as long as you are needing the brake.

The key to it all as you the travel on between A-B and A-C (fig. 36), is to be going so slowly that you create time – to think, to look all around for danger, and for all the rapid steering and straightening up that will be required.

Look in front and all around you first, to make certain you are safe to begin. Then look backwards over the left shoulder, not the right. This gives you better all round vision. But, just before the turn itself, you will need to revert your glance to look through the front and the driver's side windows for a moment, to check for traffic.

At any time there's a traffic problem either way along the road you are still leaving, it is usually best to stop. Let the others sort out what to do, rather than allowing yourself to be rushed. Remember that in the process of backing round, your offside front wing will swing out and may well cross the centre line of the road you are reversing off; therefore you must be taking account of traffic from *both* directions along it. Traffic from in front of you, in particular, would have right of way going forwards, and would hardly be expecting your wing suddenly jutting across its path.

Also note that if someone comes up wanting to emerge from the turning you are trying to reverse into, you may have to pull forward, retracing your tracks until he can do so safely; you then wait. But watch both ways before you do that, lest you pull forward into worse trouble! The other thing you have to watch all along, is that there is no-one, especially not a pint-sized person, wandering along *any* of the pavements adjacent to your manoeuvre, and who might be about to step into your path.

From the exact moment your *rear wheels* are level with an imaginary continuation of a line just inside the edge of the pavement *of the side street* (A-B as in fig. 36), you have to whisk the steering rapidly into full lock to take you round. As already warned, if your speed isn't close to zero, you will never line yourself up properly: you will over- or under-shoot.

As you begin turning, look quickly all around you to take into vision all pavements, pedestrians, children, dogs, everything! Then be looking over your left shoulder again, mainly through the back window, also through the side windows. Be prepared to stop at any stage.

A driver who is reversing must always give way to other road users from any quarter.

Once the rear of the car has begun to enter the turning, you must be ready to straighten up. You must begin to do so at just the right moment, and then do so swiftly, but without over-doing it. The right moment to begin, which will be learned through practice and is nearly always *earlier* than beginners expect, is when the back wheels of the car first reach line A-C as in fig. 36.

The front wheels need to be straight by the time they reach the line A-C.

On Test, the examiner will expect you to continue your reverse into the side street and to travel on until asked to stop. You may be allowed to stop after you have gone two car lengths from the opening, or four or five lengths, or perhaps more. Keep going 'til you are instructed to stop. The examiner wants to see that you can reverse accurately in a straight line, without wandering too far out from the pavement – or bumping into it. As you reverse on further, keep parallel to the kerb the same 3-4 tyre widths out as you were (or should have been!) when rounding the kerb on the way in.

Your examiner will indicate where you are to pull up by the kerb, well before you reach that place. (Perhaps it will be beside a lamp post, a pillar-box, or near to whatever he or she can point out that can brook no question of misunderstanding.) You should ease in towards the kerb with the same care you eased away from it at the start of the manoeuvre. Finish 1-2 tyre widths out and without hitting the kerb in the process! For your practice, make your objective to end 1 tyre width or less out from the edge. Then the Test will be easy! For your personal kerbside parking standard after you pass, never consider more than 1 tyre width to be good enough!

Reversing To The "Easy" Side
The principles and safety checks for traffic, children, etc., are identical to those explained for the "difficult" side. When to begin turning and when to straighten up are decided in the same way. Obviously it will be the right flashing indicator you use.

A major difference is that – *in addition to looking mainly over your left shoulder* – you are able to make extra checks as to just where the pavement is, over your right shoulder.

Looking over the right shoulder *only*, would be wrong, and dangerous because large areas behind and to the left of the car would remain unchecked, invisible. Nor do you merely open your door and lean out to look out of there, as is the naughty habit of lots of van drivers.

Another difference lies in which pavement you are reversing next to, having entered the limited opening. You have rounded the opening close to the right hand kerb edge. You now keep next to that edge going back. You do not try to cross to the other side of the road in reverse, before you stop. You are normally only expected to reverse a sufficient distance back, so as then to be able (with normal precautions, signal, etc.) to cross forwards, back to your own left hand side safely, and be in a proper position to emerge from the opening in due course. However, as with the left reverse, your examiner will give clear instructions about where you are to stop.

Golden Rule For Test Reverses

The golden rule for all delicate manoeuvres is that there are no medals for speed. The ability to re-capture a clutch-slipping position on the move, forwards or in reverse, is essential. See page 26. During practice sessions it is well worth stopping the car at different stages during these turns, so that you can get out and inspect just how well or badly you are really doing. On Test, although you wouldn't get out, it is in order, if necessary, to stop, if you see that you are not steering reasonably correctly or that you are about to mount a kerb. Then you can pull forward (with care!) again to straighten. You should appreciate that the examiner is more likely to mark it against you if you do hit a kerb, than if you sensibly accept your potential mistake, stop, and adjust position to avoid it.

If you do have to straighten up, there is no need to return to the original starting-off point; drive forward the minimum necessary amount. But...make sure there is no traffic first!

Choose lots of different practice venues. Find different street widths, and hilly, as well as level, terrain. Then your Test can spring no surprises! For your three-point-turns, look for spots where there aren't any roadside trees, etc., to hit...

Do remember that there are blind spots caused by the framework of your car at the front, as well as at the back. (See fig. 31.) When reversing, kids or low things like street name posts, may not be visible. In the Highway Code, you are advised to get help whenever reversing, if in any doubt; and to get out first and look, if necessary, especially if it is dark. This is extremely wise, especially if you have been parked for some while. Youngsters have a habit of sneaking up behind when you are not watching.

Safe Parking

On Test, you may be asked what precautions you would take to secure a vehicle if leaving it unattended on a hill. The answer is that you would leave the car close in, with the front wheels turned into the kerb, the handbrake "on", and in 1st or reverse gear. Engine compression resistance thus adds its holding effect to the handbrake. With automatic transmission you select the "P" position, which engages a mechanical lock, equating therefore to leaving the car in gear. You would also lock the doors against thieves, or children who might cause the car to "run away", out of control. The Highway Code carries a special section on Vehicle Security. Follow the tips given there, too.

Normally when you park, it should be on the left with the passenger side next to the kerb. (On a one-way street you may just as safely park on the right with your driver's door next to that kerb.) Signalling for pulling in to the kerb and/or parking, is described in Chapter 8. Parking in a space between two other cars at the kerbside is made easy further below.

You must heed any parking restriction. The Highway Code is effusive about where and how NOT to let your car stand. Many of the places where you are not allowed to park, are ones where you could cause an obstruction, and could be prosecuted for that anyway. Learn them – well. It also illustrates the nightmare variety of locally-sign-posted restrictions you will have to learn to obey. Among the worst offences are to park within the stud defined area around traffic lights and Pelican crossings, or inside a zigzag lined area either side of any pedestrian crossing, or less than 15 metres from any junction; also you must **not even stop to set down passengers** where any school entrance is marked, or on a clearway.

On motorways later on, once you have passed your Test and can go on them, you must remember that (apart from when directed to use the hard shoulder temporarily because of roadworks, and finding yourself on it in a stop/start queue) the only time you are permitted to stop on a hard shoulder is in emergency or if broken down. Should that happen, make sure your car is as well clear of passing traffic as you can get it; switch on your 4-way hazard warning flashers once stopped. Keep sidelights on at night. Only get out of the car via a nearside (left) passenger door. Warn all passengers to stay well off the carriageway. Detail someone to supervise children and/or animals. Make sure nobody stands about behind the car, masking your hazard and/or rear lights from traffic. Place a reflecting triangle, if you have one, on the hard shoulder 150 metres back from the car. Don't leave the car unattended for long. Summon help using the nearest roadside telephone on your own side of the motorway, or use your own car phone.

Parking At The Kerbside Between Cars
Essential though this manoeuvre is, it is not specifically required on Test, for reasons already explained. However, as a skilled driver, you should know how to do it properly.

To park in a *small* space between two other cars it is always easier to drive alongside the front car, and then reverse into the space. Trying forwards is a mistake, usually making it impossible to get close enough to the pavement. You need at least one and a half metres more than the length of your car, in order to get in.

Look at fig. 37. You are car no. 1. I assume you will have given an arm "I intend to pull in to the nearside kerb" signal if need be, as discussed on page 77, and that you will have your left flashing indicator on as you arrive.

1. Stop alongside no. 2, about two thirds of a metre out, when your *rear wheels* are level with its middle.

2. Look through the rear window, and reverse slowly, slipping the clutch. Snail it. Pull the steering wheel slightly left (left hand down) as you ease back. Keep checking for other traffic as you enter, particularly coming up from *in front* of you. Your front right wing is going to swing out, remember.

3. As the rear moves slowly into the space, increase the left hand steering wheel lock to maximum, so that your inside back wheel is aiming roughly towards the kerbstone nearest the middle of the space. Then, and this is a matter of careful judgment, as the rear snails nearer to the edge of the kerb, but before it gets there, change swiftly, completely, back onto full right lock, having a look to see that your front left wing (and the bumper) *does clear* the car in front. This is a quick look because you must still have your main attention behind. Pedestrians often attempt to walk through your space. *They assume you*

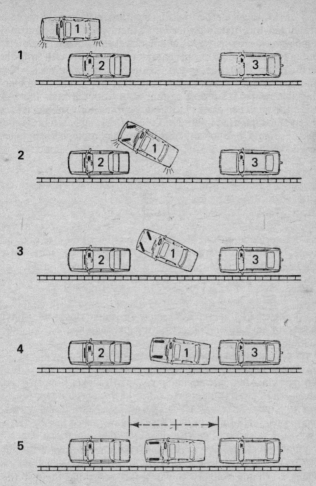

Fig. 37. Parking between cars at the kerbside.

have seen them. You may think no-one should be so daft but you would be (rightly) held responsible if you hit someone, or squashed them into the car behind. That is the law. If you have changed locks too early, stop. It's usually best to pull right forward after that and begin again.

4. Prior to your stop, pull the steering left again, in order to straighten the front wheels. Until highly practised, you may need several slow forwards and backwards manoeuvres now, in order to get your car properly under 1 car tyre width from the kerb. If car 2 is sticking too far out it can make your whole manoeuvre very difficult, but that must be no excuse for not finishing neatly the proper distance out from the kerb yourself.

5. Lastly, when close in to the edge, move forward or back, so that you occupy the middle of the available space. This leaves room to help 2 or 3, or any others who may replace them, to get in and out.

13

AUTOMATIC TRANSMISSION

As stated in Chapter 2, the law restricts people who have passed in an automatic car to driving that type only.

Types Of Fully Automatic Transmission
Models differ, so someone who understands the small details of the type you are using must help you. Most makes have two foot pedals only, and a selector in place of the normal gear lever.

The typical selector has Park, Reverse, Neutral and normal Drive positions. In addition, there may be one or more "Lock-up" gear positions, for the driver to be able to hold gears manually at times. For safety, the engine will only start in the Neutral or Park positions. This prevents the car lurching forward or back at the instant you turn the starter switch.

Driving The Car
Most of the time the Drive position is used.

You only use your RIGHT foot. You must train the left one to keep to itself!

The gears, of which there are usually only three, automatically change from 1st to 2nd, and then from 2nd to top, governed by the accelerator position, related to the workload. (The gearbox will change down, for example, for extra power going uphill.)

When you slow down, the gears change back down by themselves.

Down changes on demand, for extra acceleration, are available in Drive, via "kick down". This means pressing the accelerator pedal fully down and holding it to the floor. The gearbox changes down as far as necessary for maximum acceleration from whatever speed you were doing. It will not change down at all if you are already going faster than the pre-set maximum in the next gear down. Each gear is then held to its maximum speed before automatically changing up to the next, unless you relax the accelerator. As soon as you do that, it reverts to its normal Drive mode and, depending upon speed, this usually means it changes up directly into top at once.

The "Lock-up" provision lets you hold the transmission in low gear: e.g. Lock 1, or Lock 2. Lock 1 will hold it in 1st; in Lock 2 the gearbox will still make automatic changes but only up as far as the 2 level. If there is only one "Lock-up" position it usually equates to this Lock 2. Depending on speed, "kick-down" will usually work in Lock 2, but only within the limits of the two gears.

"Lock-up" prevents undesired upward gear changes which, in Drive, would otherwise occur. This is important for avoiding an upsetting upward change during overtaking, (see page 120), or on icy uphills (see page 187), and it should be used appropriately. "Lock-up" is essential for the engine resistance control required when descending a steep hill. (See pages 44-47.)

Normally, do not select a "Lock-up" to slow you down. From above the pre-set speed maxima, it will not engage 'til speed falls below the setting anyway. However, if your brakes fail, you must. Then, as speed drops whilst you do all else you can (see page 188), "Lock-up" will help from the first possible moment.

Park

In Park, the transmission is in neutral. The vehicle is, in addition, via the gearbox, mechanically locked against movement. You should use this position whenever you park, so that Park, as well as the handbrake, holds the car; this is vital if parked on a hill. The engine may be started, and idled or run for tuning in Park, but it should never be selected while the car is moving, which would damage the transmission.

Neutral
The out of gear position, in which you can also start the engine.

Moving Away From Rest On The Level Or Downhill
I describe this routine from the stage of having the engine running in Park or Neutral, with the handbrake still on.

First press your *right* foot on the footbrake to make certain the car is held securely. Then select Drive, keeping that footbrake on all the while; now release the handbrake. Still holding the car on the footbrake, check for safety as in Step 6 of the Smooth Take-off in Chapter 2. *Then,* when safe, and having given your signal if appropriate, you simply transfer your foot to the accelerator, so as to move off and pick up speed as required. As speed increases, Drive looks after the gear changes.

You must introduce the footbrake because, even at tick-over engine speed, the transmission begins to try to move the car once you are in Drive. Otherwise, if the tick-over setting is a touch high (or raised as it will be while the choke is operating), and/or the handbrake is a bit weak, Drive can force the car forward the instant it is engaged – before you are ready.

Slowing And Stopping
Stop the car with the footbrake. To slow the car, merely use the footbrake as required. Use "Lock-up" to add engine braking whenever going down a steep hill.

The normal thing is to leave the transmission in Drive during short stops in traffic. Other than for a steep uphill stop, when you may need the handbrake as well (see opposite), you hold the car on the footbrake. But the handbrake *should* be applied, and the gear selector returned to neutral as well, for any stops of long duration. Then you can safely remove your foot from the footbrake, and your brakelights will not stay on excessively, wearing out both their bulbs and the eyes of the driver behind – especially during rain and/or darkness. Just before you are clear to go, you get back on the footbrake, return to Drive and release the handbrake, ready to move off in the usual way.

When you reach the front line at junctions, traffic lights, roundabouts, etc., and are having to stop, then to follow that with the handbrake and returning to neutral, is again the safest technique if you have to wait long. This is because if your foot were to slip off the brake (or worse, onto the accelerator whilst you were not thinking) you will not then find yourself shot forward by mistake. This same reason makes using the handbrake and going into neutral the right policy to adopt at all pedestrian crossings, and at any stop where people are walking immediately in front of you; for example, when you are waiting in a queue and jay-walkers stray across between you and the vehicle you are stopped behind.

Manoeuvring And Reverse

People may try to persuade you to use your left foot on the brake during reversing and slow manoeuvres. It is unnecessary because slow-speed back and forward control is available with the accelerator alone (stopping with the footbrake as required). So stay with the **RIGHT FOOT ONLY** as I advocate. As a by-product, you prevent yourself ever braking and accelerating at the same time, which could be a disaster in emergency. Left foot braking – which can lead to that happening all too easily – is a dangerous, unnecessary practice, and manoeuvring is where many drivers pick up the bad habit.

Starting Uphill

Follow the same order described for "Moving Away From Rest" above. Unless the place is really quite steep, this will be fine. When it is very steep, simply leave the handbrake release until a little acceleration has been applied, and you feel the car straining a bit, rarin' to go. Then release it, and go, giving more acceleration as you do it, if you need to.

Stalling Danger

Danger can swiftly swamp you if the engine stalls (perhaps through being cold) as you are emerging from a road junction. Fast traffic coming will not be expecting you to sit in its way.

If this happens, move the selector to Neutral fast. The engine will not start in gear. Then back to Drive (or Reverse, but see page 81) to get you clear. You must practise so that this becomes a second-nature, instant, operation, otherwise you will one day find yourself in trouble.

Getting Stuck On Slippery Surfaces

"Rocking" is usually possible. Alternate selection of Drive and Reverse gears helps extract the car from being stuck in mud, snow or sand. With the engine idling to avoid damage to the transmission (don't press the accelerator), you switch from Drive to Reverse and back, with the merest split-second's delay in between. Within a couple of switches back and forth, with luck, the car will climb out one way or t'other.

PART THREE

THE DRIVING TEST

14

YOU ARE ON TEST

For the first time you, alone, are in charge. You cannot expect, nor will you receive, help from the examiner. He or she is simply there to see if you are safe, courteous, and competent to drive.

If the examiner has to pull on the handbrake, or take over the steering to avoid a collision, you must fail.

The conduct of the Driving Test is standardised throughout the country. But because you cannot quite standardise examiners, there will always be a human element. Your examiner will make the fairest judgment he or she can in passing or failing you. They all know that, because they may be called to justify their decisions, they have to observe strict Government-laid-down guidelines.

Study what you should *not* do on Test in Chapter 15.

Test application forms are obtainable from Post Offices. If there is a long waiting time in your area, you may be able to beat the queue by stating that you can take a test at short notice. But never go for one before *you* feel ready.

During your Test, remember the following "Test philosophy":

1. Although your mirrors may not show it, there is an invisible vehicle behind you, and its invisible driver is watching for your signals.

2. The vehicle immediately in front of you has a neon sign linked to its brakelights, saying, "I am going to stop – can you?".

3. Every other road user, including pedestrians, is mentally deficient, and therefore it all depends on you.

You can be certain that, on Test, the examiner will want to discover your ability to carry out a three-point-turn, a reverse into a limited opening, and an emergency stop under control. You will have to pull out from behind a parked vehicle, negotiate roundabouts, traffic lights, one-way streets, steep hill starts, pedestrian crossings of various sorts, and some difficult left and right turns. Beyond this, there is almost no limit to the sorts of road conditions your examiner may find for you.

Having a wide experience of Test conditions and requirements, I am sure Tests are conducted fairly. There are no tricks. Some examiners may be a little more exacting, but you may be certain that if on Test you give a safe exhibition of driving, even the most demanding examiner will pass you. You are either ready and fit to pass, or not. You cannot fool the examiner. He or she is not looking so much for things that you are doing correctly, as noting the things you are doing incorrectly. The examiner also wants to see whether you are confident, without showing overconfidence.

Do not worry if the examiner seems quiet, only speaking in order to issue instructions as to what you are to do next. They are not allowed to chatter, and most of them apply the rule pretty strictly.

You must have a thorough working knowledge of the Highway Code, (you will be asked questions on it like the ones I give in Chapter 16), and you must be able to read a number-plate on a stationary vehicle some 23-odd metres distant (with glasses or contact lenses if worn).

If you pass, you will be asked to sign a certificate which you will be given. This slip, combined with your provisional licence, exempts you from the necessity of "L" plates or an accompanying driver. You do not need to apply for a full licence straightaway but there is a validity time limit on these certificates, so it is best to get on with it in good time.

Nervousness

Most people are nervous on Test; some are petrified. You may not have had to take an exam for years. There is no need to be overawed, however.

The examiner realises that candidates are nervous, and makes allowances. If you are nervous, try to relax enough to prevent your nervousness affecting your driving. Sit in your seat comfortably but alert. Do not hunch up, tensed over the wheel. Don't go for your Test on an empty stomach.

It is helpful, and remarkably good for calming Test nerves, if your instructor can put you through a "trial" Test. Do it a day or two before the real one, to allow time to polish up on anything necessary. Make this last about 30-35 minutes, like the real Test, and include all the required manoeuvres.

Preparation

Make sure you know where the Test Centre is and that you get there in time. Your instructor should allow you to drive to the Centre unless it is some hugely long way away, in which event drive part way there. In winter, make sure you are warmly dressed. You may have to drive for some time with the window open to do arm signals.

Before setting off, check that your petrol tank is full, and that you have checked the condition of the tyres and their pressures. Indicators, brakelights, lights, horn, windscreen wipers and washers, brakes, steering, speedometer and all controls must function properly. Windows must be clean. Your "L" plates must be secure. A current tax "disc" has to be displayed forwards in the bottom nearside corner of the front windscreen; nowhere else will do.

Take with you, your provisional driving licence (which must be signed by you in ink), insurance certificate, vehicle M.O.T. certificate if it needs one, and Test appointment notice. *Remember your glasses or contact lenses, if worn.*

As you sit in the waiting room, use the time to do some last-minute revision of the Highway Code. That will be a whole lot more useful than worrying!

15

CHIEF REASONS FOR TEST FAILURE

Read this chapter even if you have NOT taken the Test yet.

The principal reasons for failing are always marked on a failure statement, given to you by the examiner if you are not considered up to standard. Examiners are not allowed to discuss details of why they have made their decision. Although the above sheet of paper shows you the most important reasons why you failed, it is often more difficult to see into the examiner's mind, to determine exactly why.

There may be a single specific reason. For instance, you may have disobeyed some mandatory traffic sign or broken a law. You would certainly fail if at fault on any one of numbers 1-8 below:

1. The eyesight test.
2. Failing to *give way* when obliged to, at a pedestrian crossing or at a "give-way" sign, or, failing to *stop* at a "stop" sign.
3. Causing an accident, or driving so badly that the examiner stops you, finishes the Test, gets out and tells you you may not drive on from that spot without a teacher beside you.
4. Exceeding a speed limit, except perhaps momentarily and inadvertently.
5. Going through a red traffic light.
6. Failing to do an "emergency stop" quickly and under control.

7. Emerging from any junction without due regard for approaching traffic.
8. Not keeping well to the left while driving along, other than when driving appropriately using an outer lane for the time being, or in a one-way street when you needed a right hand lane.

A combination of two or more of the principal faults 9-20 below is also likely to result in failure:

9. Bad positioning, and inadequate signalling.
10. Insufficient use of the mirrors.
11. Speeds unsuited to conditions – too fast, or, slow.
12. Lane indiscipline.
13. Inability to answer most of the simple questions on the Highway Code which you will be asked.
14. Misuse or poor use of any major control.
15. Slipping back on a hill start.
16. Not being able to reverse accurately and safely into, and then backwards along, a limited opening.
17. Not being able to do a three-point-turn, safely, and without bumping the kerbs.
18. Lack of courtesy shown to other road users.
19. Not leaving enough clearance when passing stationary – or moving – vehicles, especially cyclists.
20. Lack of awareness of other road users.

There are marginal causes of Test failure, where you may not have performed any of the "crimes" listed above, but where the examiner still feels that you are not sufficiently experienced to be allowed to drive on your own. For instance, you may have repeatedly rushed up behind stationary traffic, and then been forced to brake sharply. You may have "dithered": at roundabouts, traffic lights, etc., you may repeatedly have delayed moving on when it was safe, showing undue hesitation, and causing harassment to traffic behind. It may have been a combination of many small things which it is perhaps difficult to put a finger on, but the examiner is in no doubt that he or she must fail you.

16

SOME QUESTIONS WHICH MAY BE ASKED BY EXAMINERS

Before you can be awarded a Test pass, the examiner has to ask some questions to test your knowledge of the rules of the road. He needs to be sure you understand the Highway Code and that you will be able to cope with motorways as soon as you are allowed to drive on them. You will not necessarily fail if you get one question wrong, but if you get the majority wrong it is bound to count against you, even if your driving is first-class. Test your knowledge on the typical questions below: the answers start on page 156. *

1. What does the Highway Code say about signals from other people and other drivers?
2. What is the Highway Code?
3. What should you *not* do when being overtaken?
4. What should you study in the Highway Code other than specific rules for drivers?
5. What precautions would you take if you parked a car at night on your offside?
6. What should you consider if you see a 'bus waiting at a 'bus stop? What should you consider when you see a moving 'bus?

* These are only a few of the possible questions that examiners may ask. For a much larger selection, consult "Highway Code Questions and Answers" by John Humphries, a companion book in the Paperfronts series.

7. What is the meaning of white lines on the road?

8. When should you *not* use your headlights at night?

9. How would you arm signal to a policeman the direction you wish to take?

10. What is the meaning and the sequence of traffic signal lights?

11. When can you pass a red light?

12. When are you compelled to stop?

13. Which sign means priority over approaching vehicles?

14. How must you control your speed?

15. What does the Highway Code say about entering or leaving roadside property?

16. What should you do if you stall, break down, or have an accident on an automatic half-barrier level crossing?

17. What does the Highway Code say about parking in relation to traffic signs?

18. You may come across a gantry above a motorway, which carries white arrows pointing vertically down and facing some of the lanes. What do they mean?

19. What is shown on the "Level Crossing, No Gates" road sign?

20. Is there any significance to the length of the broken white lines down the centre of the road?

21. What is the difference between broken and continuous double white lines down the centre of a road?

22. Name six occasions when it is imperative that you check first in your driving mirrors.

23. Name two special times to avoid pulling in to the left.

24. How would you travel in convoy?

25. What is the routine Highway Code motto for every major change of course?

26. How many days are you allowed in which to produce to the police, when required, your driving licence, a valid certificate of insurance for the car, and an M.O.T. test certificate for it if it needs one?

27. What would you do if involved in an accident with any third party (person, animal as listed in the Highway Code, vehicle or property)?

28. If you run over a dog do you report it to the police?

29. What precautions should you take before opening any door of your vehicle?

30. How would you travel in daylight, or night-time, fog?

31. What should you remember about speed at night?

32. Besides the police, who else has authority to control traffic?
33. What does the Highway Code say about overtaking when you are within the zigzag lined area on the approach to a zebra or pedestrian crossing?
34. Describe the "school" sign.
35. What is the ideal instance to stop behind another vehicle in a queue?
36. In a moving stream of traffic, what is a safe distance to follow the vehicle in front?
37. When can driving become unsafe on a motorway?
38. What should you do if anything falls from your vehicle?
39. What is a clearway?
40. Can you ever cross a cycle lane, or drive along one?
41. What do the series of signs which are circular, and have white symbols on a solid blue background, generally give you?
42. Can one turn right directly off a motorway?
43. If you have a puncture or breakdown on a motorway, what do you do?
44. How do you overtake a slow-moving car which hugs the centre of a road?
45. Small red or white markers (mounted on low black and white posts) reflect well at night to tell you what?
46. As a rule, what does the shape of a road sign mean?
47. Describe the "no overtaking" sign.
48. Describe the "no motor vehicles" sign.
49. On motorways at night, you will observe amber-coloured studs, red studs and green studs, rather like the white cat's eyes. What does each type of colour stud mean?
50. If you can't always remember the detail of a road sign, then knowing the *principle* upon which it would have been drawn can help. Can you think of one such principle?
51. How much is it *safe* to drink and drive?
52. Is there an assumed speed limit in a built-up area?
53. What is a U turn?
54. Who has right of way at an unmarked junction or crossroads?
55. Can you just slow down when *you* feel like it, and pull into the kerb on a whim?

56. Do some cars have more powerful brakes than others?
57. When *must* you have headlights on at night?
58. What should you do if a dog runs in front of you?
59. Is there a national speed limit?
60. How do you treat railway level crossings?
61. There are times when you are not allowed to sound your horn. When are they?
62. Picture an up-and-down-dale sort of country route. What should you do when approaching a dip in the road, sufficiently deep to conceal trouble which won't be seen 'til you arrive?
63. What should you do when *not* approaching such a dip in the road?
64. What should you be careful to avoid with your brakes on wet nights?
65. What should a driver know about first aid?
66. Imagine that, at a junction where you must give way, your direction will be straight across the major road. There is room for two lanes on your side at the neck of your present road. Which is the preferable one to use?
67. What must you *not* do with rear fog lights?
68. If you were travelling in the left lane along an otherwise empty dual carriageway, how might you help a driver waiting at the left (at the only turning in sight), to join it?
69. Can you cross a 'bus lane during its hours of operation, in order to reach a side road or access property?

Answers

1. Watch for them, and take any necessary action promptly.
2. The Highway Code is a booklet checked and passed by Parliament for the guidance of all road users. Whilst Courts have a due regard for it, it is not, itself, the law.
3. You should not accelerate or pull out to the offside. (Slow down if necessary.)
4. The rules all the other road users are meant to obey. You should know what rules to expect that they will (in theory!) follow.
5. Other than in a one-way street, you must turn the car round so that it faces the same direction as the traffic. At

night, you also normally have to leave the sidelights on. However, although you are advised NOT to park on major roads, where a road has a speed limit of 30 m.p.h. (or less) you may park without lights, so long as you park close to the kerb and at least 15 metres from any junction, and so that you will not be breaking any of the very many other waiting and parking rules given in the Highway Code.

6. Be prepared to allow the 'bus to move out should it indicate readiness to pull out. Watch for passengers walking out (or children running) from around the 'bus. In town traffic, the Highway Code goes further. It decrees that you "...**give way to 'buses indicating an intention to move out from 'bus stops if you can do so safely".** When you see a moving 'bus, watch out for passengers who may be stupid enough to try to jump off before it stops.

7. Lines at right angles across the road, indicate the "stop" or the "give-way" point for vehicles at junctions. Double white centre lines are explained in question 21.

Broken white lines and/or cat's-eye studs in the middle, parallel with the kerb, mean "keep to the left", and separate the traffic going each way. Extra, lane discipline dividing lines may be painted where more than one lane in each direction is intended. Keep in the left lane unless overtaking, or if arrows on the road indicate some other correct lane for your direction.

Where a *two-way* road has *three* lanes, keep in the left one. The centre lane, as explained on page 125 is for overtaking or turning right only. If you are overtaking, look out! Should there be someone ahead, also apparently overtaking in the same direction as you, stay well back from that vehicle. If you both have to move in more suddenly than you planned – will there be a gap (or gaps) for both of you? If it turns out the driver in front is not intending to overtake as you thought but is really slowing down preparatory to turning right, are you going to be "snookered" behind him or her, unable to move in, and then dangerously exposed in that fast middle lane?

On dual carriageways there may be two, three, and occasionally more, lanes in your direction, divided by broken lane lines. Always use the left lane unless you are passing slower traffic. Only move out the least number of lanes you need to (having regard to your mirrors) when you wish to pass someone. Do not normally use an outer lane if the one next on your left is clear. To drive slowly along, blocking a lane when one to your left is clear, deliberately or absent-mindedly holding up people behind who want to overtake, is a prosecutable obstruction offence.

Theoretically, the lanes nearest the outside should be empty most of the time because all drivers should follow the rule just described, as laid down in the Highway Code. That they frequently do not, is one of the prime causes of frustration, and of the multi-storey pile-ups that frequently hit the news headlines. It is shameful that our police do not do more about these mobile obstructors.

8. When the car is parked.
9. (1) Turning right: right arm, straight outside the car, palm of the hand facing forwards.
   (2) Straight on: left arm vertical from the elbow, inside the car, fingers pointing towards top of windscreen.
   (3) Turning left: left arm and fingers outstretched horizontally, palm forward, inside the car.
   In (2) and (3) above, get your arm as close to the screen as you can, but do not touch it with greasy fingers. Mind your examiner's nose!
10. Red light means "stop".
    Red-and-amber means "stop", or remain stopped.
    Green light means "go" if safe.
    Amber light alone means "stop" – you may only go on if you have crossed the stop line, or are so close to it that to pull up might cause an accident.
    Sequence, is red, red-and-amber, green, amber, red.
11. When a separate green "filter" arrow is showing at the same time: you may go if safe but in the arrowed direction only!
12. Whenever not to (or at least to try your best to) would lead unavoidably to your being part of an accident; if involved in an accident; when requested to do so by traffic controllers; at a "stop" sign; for police; to allow pedestrians free passage on an uncontrolled pedestrian crossing; at a Pelican crossing light when the colour(s) demand it; at steady amber, or twin flashing red, railway

level crossing lights; at an amber, or a red, or a red and amber traffic light.

13. A blue square with a thin white border; a large white arrow on the left side points up and a red arrow (smaller) on the right points down.

14. Speed must never rise above that from which *you will be able to pull up safely, well within the distance which you can see is clear ahead;* circumstances and weather must be taken into account. Nor may you ever brake sharply, *except in an emergency.* You must also obey speed limits.

15. Give way to *pedestrians* on any pavement, as well as to traffic on the road. Pavements are for people – not motor vehicles.

16. If you cannot re-start, or somehow go, **immediately**, then try to get clear by driving "on the starter" in first gear (not possible with automatic transmission) – otherwise, FIRST get your passengers out and clear of the crossing. **NEXT** phone the signalman at once, using the phone provided.

    THEN, only if there is time, push the car clear. Let the signalman know if you succeed BUT stand well out of the way if the alarm gongs sound and the amber lights come on, or the twin red flashing lights begin.

17. You may not park where your vehicle would obscure a traffic sign (including signs painted on the carriageway).

18. A white downward-pointing arrow facing you above a lane means you may use that lane. These gantries also carry **X** (cross) signs in red, facing the traffic above lanes which are closed. You must move, with care, out of an **X**'d lane into a clear lane, well before you reach an **X** sign.

19. An old-type steam engine in black on a white background, within a red triangle.

20. Yes. The broken lines are made longer and the gaps shorter, on the approach side of any hazard, such as the brow of a hill.

21. You may not cross a continuous double white line, or one with the continuous line on your side (except to pass a stationary obstruction). Where the left line nearest you is broken, you may cross it, *if safe.* Parking is banned wherever there are double white lines, whichever side

you might be contemplating it.
22. When you are about to:
1) Stop (or slow).
2) Move off from the side of the road (look round as well).
3) Turn right or left; double-check just before you turn.
4) Overtake.
5) Open a door on either side to get out of the car (best to look round too).
6) Change lane.
23. When turning right. When alongside a 'bus lane, or a cycle lane, to your left.
24. With sufficient distance between your vehicle and the one in front, for a faster overtaking vehicle to move in between. (Note that for safety, and so that the party should have little trouble keeping together, the fastest vehicles/drivers should always be at the back of a convoy.)
25. **Mirrors – Signal – Manoeuvre.**
26. Seven.
27. STOP. Unless too injured yourself, initiate action to prevent more people running into the accident parties. Make sure all engines are switched off and nobody is smoking. See that any First Aid needed is begun promptly and that further help, if required, is being called. (You should know, at the least, the brief first aid given in your Highway Code.) Then, if able, *get and give* the required information shown in the Highway Code. If there is damage or injury (including that to most animals), you must produce your current certificate of insurance, *at the time,* to the police or to anyone with reasonable grounds for requiring to see it. If this has not been done, the accident must be reported to the police inside 24 hours, and the certificate (not a photocopy) must be shown to the police at any convenient police station inside seven days. Note that police can also require production of a valid vehicle M.O.T. certificate when applicable.

The author suggests: get name(s) and address(es) of the other driver(s) involved, registration number(s) of the other vehicle(s), the name(s) of their insurance company(ies) and the addresses of as many witnesses as you can. In a serious accident take road measurements. Your insurance policy also probably tells you not to admit blame. (It may not be your fault!)

28. Yes, inside 24 hours, unless, at the time, you have given the information required.

29. Make sure (look round) that no-one on the road, pavement or footpath is likely to run into the door. Cyclists are particularly vulnerable. Passengers should get out on the side nearer the kerb if possible. *You* are responsible for controlling children in this regard.

30. Day or night – with dipped headlights or a pair of front fog lights on; and with sidelights showing at the back – or much better, with a rear fog light or lights *as well* (but these must only be on when visibility is seriously reduced); AND observing the Fog Code which forms part of the Highway Code. Learn the Fog Code. See also page 172.

31. Never go above a speed from which you would be unable to stop safely, well within the range of your headlights' vision.

32. People in charge of roadworks (with red and green flags or signs); street crossing patrols; traffic wardens; *anybody* who temporarily has to do so.

33. **"... you must not overtake the moving motor vehicle nearest the crossing, or the leading vehicle which has stopped to give way to a pedestrian...".**

34. Two children (in a hurry), black on white, within a red triangle.

35. Up to half a car length behind.

36. One Highway Code recommendation is to leave a gap of about one metre for each mile per hour you are travelling. I advise you to allow more, especially if traffic ahead is moving bunched rather than well-spaced. On wet roads, treble that. On snow or ice, ten times can be insufficient! Another Code suggestion is to allow a two-second time-gap. Watch the vehicle ahead pass a lamp-post or conspicuous mark; say slowly under your breath, "one second, two seconds". If you reach that mark before there is time to say it all, you are too close. Try it!

The pressure of congestion is turning many major routes into "moving traffic jams" which hurtle nose-to-tail at 70 m.p.h. (and more!). The slightest hold-up causes an instant tail-back jam, miles long. Shunts and even major pile-ups, unrelated to the original stoppage, are common. Accident potential multiplies sharply if a tail-back grows topsy, back towards a bend or brow of a hill. This is because the last to arrive around the bend or over the brow, are so often going faster at that crucial moment, than would conceivably have allowed them to stop *within the distance they could see to be clear.* Driving too close is always blamed, but I also believe drivers fail to look far enough ahead up the traffic stream, and to slow-up *immediately* that long view shortens. See Commandments 8, 9 and 10, from page 169, and page 127.

37. When there is an accident in front; if some fallen load lies on the carriageway; in fog; in high cross-winds; in teeming rain compounded by wheel-spray; in snow or ice; when flashing "panel" signs carry any lit-up message – speed limit, direction arrow, lane closure, etc.; wherever there are roadworks, and especially where there are contra-flow lanes; if you are tired.

38. Except on motorways, stop as soon as you safely can, and with due care remove the article from the road. On motorways, use the nearest roadside telephone to inform the police. Do not attempt to retrieve any object yourself.

39. A stretch of road where, except in emergency or breakdown, or in a traffic queue, no stopping whatsoever is allowed on the carriageway; you mustn't even pull in to consult a map.

40. It is illegal to drive along, or park on, a cycle lane which is marked by a solid (continuous) white line. If you have to cross one you must look out, first, for any cycles using it. If the lane is marked by a broken line, the rule is slightly less stringent. You are only asked to "avoid" driving or parking on the lane (not that you would anyway), but you must be equally careful if you need to cross it.

41. Positive instructions; e.g. "Ahead only".

42. No. You always leave a motorway via a slip-road at the left.

43. Get your car on the "hard shoulder" having previously looked in your mirrors and signalled, if possible. You are now in danger. Think, before you try to telephone for help. See my warnings on page 173.

44. Toot gently and/or flash headlights to let the driver know you are there. Wait until it is safe to pass. Slower drivers *should move over* as much as they can as soon as they

can.

45. Red ones on the left, white ones on the right, help you pick out the edges of suddenly narrow or bending parts of the road.

46. Usually: circular signs are mandatory, triangular signs warn, and rectangular signs give direction information.

47. Red circle enclosing black car and red car side by side, on white background. The red car is on the right to denote the warning.

48. Red circle enclosing black motorbike above black car, on white background.

49. Amber-coloured studs mark the right hand edge of the motorway. Red studs mark the left hand edge. Green studs separate acceleration/deceleration lanes from the through carriageway. Note: some of these studs are now also used on major trunk roads of near motorway standard.

50. Red colouring of a symbol on a sign or across part of one, normally denotes the negative aspect of that sign – i.e. which drivers are not allowed to do something, which lane has less priority or cannot be used, and so on; look at, for example, "No overtaking", "Priority over vehicles from opposite direction", "No through road".

51. Never drink before driving. It is most dangerous and even a small amount of drink may raise your blood-alcohol count above the limit. At best you might lose your licence, at worst you might kill someone. If severe damages have had to be paid, you may also find yourself taken to Court by your insurance company, and that you may then stand to lose everything you own.

52. Yes. Wherever there are street-lamps the limit will be 30m.p.h. unless small repeat signs indicate a higher speed.

53. Only possible if a road is wide enough and gaps in the traffic both ways allow it .This means swinging round in one ∩ swoop to go the other way. A special sign sometimes prohibits U turns. Obviously they are illegal in a one-way street! Pull up on the left first, to wait for a traffic-free moment. Allow enough "safe" time in case you misjudge the width, and have to reverse a little, before you can get round.

54. There are quite a few junctions where it would be very difficult to say with certainty. Be prepared to give way.

By far the best plan is always to treat the other road as if it is the major road.

55. No. You will see people doing this so they can dash in and get cigarettes from a shop: you will see them doing it for no reason you can understand. It is dangerous. It shows that the person either has no idea who may be in their mirrors, or could not care who is there anyway. It is your responsibility to select a safe position whenever you pull in, and to do so giving reasonable warning to other people, i.e. slowing down gently after signalling your intention.

56. Yes. Many cars now have "anti-lock" braking. See page 32.

57. The basic rules I give in Chapter 19, under **"Night Driving"**. You should understand that, apart from where good street lighting may permit you to travel on sidelights alone, YOU MUST HAVE HEADLIGHTS ON at night. (No dousing them when behind someone on an unlit country road...you will see people do it!) The exception above does *not* apply to a motorway, however well lit. On motorways at night, headlights must *always* be on when you are moving.

58. A dog cannot be regarded as important enough to swerve for, if doing so will cause another, greater, accident. Obviously try to stop if at all possible, but bear in mind human(e) priorities.

59. For cars, at the time of writing, it is 70 m.p.h. on dual carriageways and on motorways. On single carriageways it is 60 m.p.h. The sign for the end of any lower speed limit, which is a plain white circle with a diagonal black line across it from bottom left to top right, therefore really means that the appropriate "national" limit applies thereafter, 'til you next reach another lower speed limit. You also need to know about the different national speed limits, given in the Highway Code, which apply to a car if you have a trailer, and which are applied to the various other types of vehicle.

60. When an accident happens on a level crossing, someone usually dies. The rules are unfortunately extensive, but must all be taken seriously. Learn them from the Highway Code.

61. In built-up areas at night (11.30 p.m. to 7.00 a.m.), or, when you are stationary – unless some other vehicle is

about to hit you.

62. Slow down sufficiently, to be able to stop, whatever you might find in that dip which could cause you to have to do so.

63. Look out for a concealed dip! Being an infrequent hazard they are death traps. There ought to be a specific sign for them; amazingly, there isn't.

64. Avoid keeping your foot on the footbrake at traffic hold-ups, if it will mean your brakelights dazzling those waiting behind unnecessarily. Save them eye-strain.

65. Even if you have had formal training, look at the special section in the Highway Code where priorities are also suggested. One day it may be your turn to be glad someone did...

66. If someone in front of you is turning right, use the left hand one. However, if the right hand lane is free, you can use it, even though the left one is usually thought of as the "natural" choice. Doing so, leaves the left one open for those who want to turn left to be getting on, despite your maybe having to wait before going across. (The same point applies as you leave a twin-laned one-way street.) When the majority of a bunch of traffic reaching the junction are wanting to turn left, this "thinking drivers'" lane choice, helps traffic-flow.

67. You must not use them at any time other than when visibility is *seriously* reduced. According to the Highway Code, that situation prevails only when you cannot see beyond 100 metres. At night, or in clear rain, you must not dazzle people behind deliberately, or by clean forgetting to turn them off once a need has passed. Such forgetfulness is an all too common source of dangerous dazzle for everyone behind. You should know which dashboard warning light it is, which reminds you they are "ON".

68. Double-check your mirrors, and, if safe, signal and move over to the right hand lane. Provided anyone behind you does the same, this should make it possible for the waiting driver to move out sooner – at his or her own risk!

69. Yes: with the same care you would cross or turn through any other major road lane. When turning right, this amounts to the normal rule of the road, whereby you **give way to oncoming traffic.** When you are turning left, the

law is less clear. Suppose you are in a lane next outside to a 'bus lane, moving slowly, and indicating to turn left. Should a 'bus lane user then dare to rattle past you on the inside – regardless? Since the Highway Code says to you, **"look out"**, for any vehicle in a 'bus lane, perhaps the answer is a definite maybe, that they can, despite all other bans on overtaking on the inside. I suggest, therefore, that whatever the rights or wrongs may be, you are particularly careful never to clash with any 'bus lanester, even ones using the lane illegally. Give Way. If you are having to cross a 'bus lane on your left to get into a road, move into the lane comfortably before the turning itself. That will be safer than trying to cross it sharply. Beware! Some of these lanes are "contra-flow", running the opposite way to that you expect!

NOTES

(You may like to jot down here, favourite questions which come up in your area, about which your instructor can advise you.)

17

SUMMING UP FOR LEARNERS

Although as an "L" you are not allowed on motorways, you may be asked about them. So please read Chapter 18. I also hope that you will study carefully the final chapter on more advanced driving. It illustrates a few of the secrets that are second-nature to the really competent driver, and explains skidding. For all your driving days, please remember that your car is lethal – it can kill.

Here are my "Ten Commandments".

Ten Commandments

1. Concentrate.
2. Be courteous to other users of the road. (For example, give room when being passed.)
3. Watch road surfaces constantly. (See next two chapters.)
4. When in doubt, DON'T RISK IT.
5. Never travel faster than you can think.
6. Never take your eyes off the road, or argue with passengers.
7. Stepping on the gas kills more than inhaling it. Better later here than earlier hereafter! Hasten if you like, but never rush.
8. Whenever behind another vehicle, constantly maintain your position – within the confines of lane discipline and keeping to your own side of the road – for the best view round ahead of him. Hold your braking gap, ever sufficient. Following close-up (nose-to-tail) and exactly in someone's tracks, is a death recipe.
9. In making your No. 8, above, thinking, instinctive,

remember always **to relate position and speed to danger.** Immediately congestion or a hazard ahead is suspected, slow down, so as to lengthen your braking space and open up your view. Only when you know it is clear dare you allow yourself closer. Do not be pressurised by bumper-to-bumperists, hard on your tail. When your sixth sense says "slow up", SLOW UP. If there isn't room for you to maintain your one door's (wide!) opening width away, as you pass parked vehicles, without getting closer to oncoming vehicles than the parked ones, **cut your speed right down instead** – *to walking pace if necessary.* Then, if a sudden stop is forced upon you, you can do it.

10. Take the long view ahead constantly, as well as the near view in front. Whenever your driving horizon shortens, slash your speed accordingly. *The faster you go, the further ahead you must be certain there will be no complications.* Look long, live long.

PART FOUR

AFTER YOUR TEST

18

MOTORWAYS

Lane Discipline

Never, no matter how many lanes, overtake on the left. *This is illegal,* except to avoid a crash, or if congestion causes queuing and your "inside" lane happens to move first. The fact that you may be leaving the motorway via a slip road shortly, does not give you permission to suddenly accelerate up the inside left lane before you reach the slip. You must not "buzz" a middle lane driver who is travelling freely along catching up left-lane traffic he or she intends to pass, and frighten that driver in this way.

On a two-lane motorway drive in the left hand lane. You only use the right hand lane for overtaking.

On a three-lane motorway, normally drive on the left hand lane, but if there is a lot of slow-moving traffic on it, then travel in the middle lane while passing them. There is no need to "leap-frog" in and out between each left lane vehicle. That could cause unnecessary danger. However, you must return to the left lane whenever it is clear for a decent distance. And it would be sensible to move into a gap midway past a long line of left lane traffic, if necessary to let anyone consistently too close to your tail, pass through. The right lane is *only for overtaking traffic in the middle lane.* (See also Question 7 on page 154.)

Aquaplaning

A principal skidding danger on a motorway, and on all "fast" roads, is known as aquaplaning. On a wet surface, as speed rises, a wedge of water builds up underneath the front tyres. Up to 70 m.p.h. on a wet surface, the effect is not usually noticeable unless tyre treads are badly worn down; much over that speed, and the front wheels will, in the wet, begin to skim the water surface. When this terrifying phenomenon takes hold, steering control disappears, although the driver may not realise what has happened until too late. A gust of wind, an unexpected bump, or an attempt to steer, and the car could instantly be on its way, spinning toward death.

You will often see a fine skin of water laying across a motorway carriageway during the worst of a downpour. This happens in a few places where the water cannot run away quickly enough, off a badly drained surface. If you hit one of these "ponds" of water, even at 50-60 m.p.h., the drag created by the water can have an horrendous aquaplaning effect – particularly if only one side of the car hits it. Grip the steering tightly to keep straight. Come off your accelerator, so that your water-skiing car sinks back to the road surface, and safety, just as fast it can.

The sure way to prevent aquaplaning is:
   a)   Have correctly inflated tyres with plenty of tread.
   b)   Keep below 70 m.p.h. on wet, and slow up for "ponds".
Aquaplaning danger is not removed just because you may have a fast car. *It applies equally to all.*

Fog

Motorway fog seems to bring out many insane drivers who drive too fast. Such "motoring mania" is believed to be partly caused by a false sense of security building up, due to drivers being deprived of any natural speed judgment mechanism; that is, through losing touch with any feeling of speed derived from seeing the surrounding countryside flash past. It would appear that people at the wheel, instead, try mistakenly to judge their speed in relation to other vehicles. Their own speed is then invariably *much too fast.*

The result is the wall-to-wall motorway carnage which causes so much damage, injury and grief. Check-in to your speedometer, not into the back of the car in front.

In thick fog, my advice is to get off the motorway, or you may become involved in an accident through no fault of your own. If you have to drive on, make sure your windscreen wipers and interior de-mister are on at full *hot* blast whenever necessary, otherwise you can find half the trouble is on your own windscreen. And follow the "Fog Code". Please read that section of your Highway Code *now.* See also Question 30, page 154.

In bad fog you are fortunate if you come across a police car going your way. The driver should set a safe pace based on police knowledge gained from the bitter experience of cleaning up previous tragedies. Keep well back, nevertheless. Overtake, and you are likely to be prosecuted!

Warning Signs On A Motorway

Blue flashing police lights forewarn of smashes...if they get there before you.

Various fixed carriageway lights (see Highway Code) may be lit to alert you before you reach fog, roadworks, or snowy or icy road conditions. You are warned to slow down and proceed with extreme caution. Temporary speed limits marked by normal signs must be obeyed.

When "up-and-down" amber lights (mounted one above the other) are flashing alternately, you should keep under 30 m.p.h. (slower if circumstances dictate), 'til you see conditions are clear. If an advisory speed is lit up on a panel type sign, stay under that limit. But do not assume the speed is safe just because it is on the panel. Go slower if necessary. Indeed, you can never assume the speed drivers in front of you may be going is necessarily safe, can you?

Breakdowns On Motorways

If you break down, get your car on to the hard shoulder. Telephones, from which you may call for help, are provided at intervals, and arrow posts about every 100 metres point the way to the nearest one on your side. (Don't even consider crossing to the other carriageway.) Take care though! See page 142. Stopping on the hard shoulder except for emergency or breakdown *is illegal.*

Entering And Leaving A Motorway

Apart from the ends of a motorway, where there may be a roundabout, or a dual carriageway may simply become a motorway, you can only enter a motorway along a "slip road". This is an extra lane at the entry point, running alongside the left lane of the motorway. It is provided so that you can build up speed on it. This should enable you to match your speed with vehicles on the motorway inside lane, before you move out into a safe gap in the traffic. Use right flashing indicator for merging on. Keep it on until you leave the slip road. Glance over your right shoulder, as well as watching in your mirrors, so as to see properly the traffic bearing down upon you along the motorway. Get on to the inside lane at the first safe opportunity. *Try not to drive to the end of the "slip road" and then stop. If you cannot* slot in behind someone, "time it", instead, by going slowly *at first*, until you see a gap in the left lane traffic to accelerate and merge into. If you do ever have to stop, you then must wait for a *very* much larger gap. It takes a long time to accelerate from scratch to a motorway speed.

There are two traps to be wary about during the merging on process, especially on a very busy motorway.

1. Others in front of you also trying to merge on may come to an abrupt halt, either through mis-timing or because of a sheer lack of a chance to go. Beware you don't run into them because you are too busy observing behind, trying to assess your own merge.

2. A vehicle overtaking inside-lane traffic on the motorway may be moving *in* towards the same gap you are expecting to merge *out* into! So you have more than one lane to watch... (Note that, once you're on the motorway, if you wish to move out to a middle lane to overtake, you have a similar problem to watch for, with outside lanesters moving in.)

Leaving a motorway, reduce your speed and get into the inside lane in good time. Blue background count-down markers, marked **III, II** and **I**, indicate that you are getting near to your slip road. Move gradually into the slip road from the very beginning of it. Use your left flashing indicator when leaving the motorway.

These methods of entering and leaving apply both at intermediate access points and service areas. You would use similar methods before and after a breakdown stop on the hard shoulder. At the end of a motorway there are plenty of warning signs, but see **Speed** below.

Sleep

If you are prone to drowsiness, do not take risks. Turn off at the next access point or service area, and rest. Until you reach it, open the window for bursts of fresh air, and drive extremely carefully. If you really have no time to stop for a nap, then, before going on any further than necessary, leave the motorway and get out and walk around, or better still, run around, to wake yourself up. Have a fizzy drink, for zest. You must be ("alive" –) honest with yourself about whether you are safe, before taking the wheel again.

Petrol

At high motorway speeds petrol burns quicker. Watch you do

not run out. Service areas are some distance apart, and you pay heavily for someone to bring it to you.

At a few motorway places, such as on elevated urban ones, there is no hard shoulder due to the expense or impossibility of building one. To run out of petrol in such a place is a grave hazard to other motorists. When approaching these areas, instinctively double-check your fuel gauge.

Lane Changing And Overtaking

See the motorway section of the Highway Code. Never swing suddenly to another lane, either inwards or outwards. Watch your mirrors, signal the change briefly when safe; move over gradually. With an abrupt lurch at speed you might lose control, causing an accident.

Whereas we earlier noted that a signal for moving in, after overtaking, is rarely useful, on a motorway it *is* an important one to give. People being passed will not otherwise know you intend to move in straightaway.

You may also have a problem, when moving back into a middle lane, in that someone on a lane inside that, is trying to move out, into the same gap! That driver should cede you priority but you can't count on it. Your signal helps him or her realise your intention. This is simply the reverse of the problem described above as trap 2, when you enter a motorway.

As lane changes require very little steering wheel movement, your flashing indicator cancelling habit (see page 70) must be in full play.

Although the national speed limit applies on motorways, many people break the law, and drive much faster. If you swing out suddenly, you give such a speeding overtaker no chance. That driver should not break the law and should be more careful, as explained on page 128, but in the event of an accident the main fault would be yours.

When you yourself want to overtake, start with your mirrors and then your signal, and then carry out the manoeuvre with the usual care. The advice I give in Chapter 11 under **Overtaking On Dual Carriageways** is vital. Please read it again. Assessing the situation in your mirrors *over a long enough period to be certain what is there* is of paramount importance. Mirrors' blind spots (fig. 31) can provide no excuse for being too hasty.

Changing Direction On A Motorway

If you miss your turn-off point you have got to go on to the next.

It is illegal to turn across the central reservation. If you are alone, check your exit number before getting onto the motorway. You cannot stop on the hard shoulder to check...

Roadworks

Motorway roadworks are, unfortunately, common. Closing of a lane or even two lanes, is a serious hazard to fast-moving traffic, so you are normally given long-distance warning. The usual sign is the "lane closed" sign shown in the Highway Code, given in electric "wicket" form, with flashing yellow lights above and below to alert you. Slow and prepare to be "funnelled" into the clear lane(s). The police switch on the flashing lights, but if they fail, the first hint you get may be an ordinary roadworks sign, or a diversion notice, so keep awake. As a rule, red and white cones mark off the way, but if *you* will have to change lanes, you should move across well before these are reached. Such a lane change is akin to joining the motorway from a slip road, insofar as that drivers already in a clear lane at the point the roadworks are reached, take priority. Well before that point, you must allow time to merge over without danger to those drivers, or you can be "pinned" to a halt by the time you reach the cones.

You must heed these warnings, sometimes exasperating if there is a long queue, and take your turn, not trying to "beat anyone to it". Use the hard shoulder if so instructed.

Contra-flow lanes, where you are diverted to the opposing carriageway (or vice versa), are obviously very dangerous. The statistics prove it, too, and that they are worst in inclement weather, so keep awake and observe all temporary signs and speed limits.

Speed

The maximum speed allowed on motorways and dual carriageways is 70 m.p.h. On certain urban motorways, a lower speed limit is in operation, shown by signs.

Whenever slowing up for your exit point, or if all traffic ahead has slowed right down or stopped, it is essential not to be fooled about how fast you are still going. Prolonged spells at speed make ordinary speeds seem like a ridiculous crawl; 60 m.p.h. feels like 20 m.p.h. Even long experienced drivers check, by looking at the speedometer, that speed *is* low enough for the slip road or the end of the motorway.

The Ten Commandments of Chapter 17 all apply to motorway driving. "Look long, live long", especially, applies with a vengeance because of everyone's high speeds. You may not be able to pick out individual vehicles on your forward horizon, but if you see the general flow is being interrupted, ease off *instantly*. You can always press on when you see it's clear; but if a stoppage happens, you may well have no chance of stopping safely if you haven't taken that "instant" advice. Provided you have, then whatever level of progressive braking may be needed, should be safely within your grasp.

The "slow lorries for XX mile(s)" sign is one of the smallest, but most important, signs on the motorway. A silhouetted lorry climbing a steep slope is pictured in black on a white background inside a red triangle, with appropriate wording carried on a plate below. This sign presages deep trouble whenever the motorway is carrying thick traffic. Take notice when you see one. As soon as the slowest lorries start to crawl, the middle lane finds a sudden influx of other left lane traffic, simply wanting to maintain their speed by moving out. The effect "knocks on" in a similar way with middle lane traffic barging out into the outer lane(s). The scene is set for a completely unexpected (by all who ignored the sign – i.e. 80% of drivers) rapid tailgate build-up, and possible all-lane stoppage. That is why motorway hills, often unnoticeable to the driving-eye (i.e. without the sign), are such accident black-spots. The smashes nearly always happen at the rear, miles back from the uphill itself.

When travelling for long motorway distances at speed, keep an eye on your oil pressure gauge or warning light, as well as the coolant temperature gauge. It is wise to check the coolant level before your journey. A comparatively small fault, such as water pump failure, can cause expensive overheating damage if the car is driven far at speed before a defect is noticed.

19

THE MORE ADVANCED DRIVER

The advanced driver differs from the learner in many ways. Let's watch Jack and Jill, in turn, both of them lifelong safe drivers.

Sometimes Jack's anticipation appears to be psychic! Suddenly you find that he has been slowing, in control, more than you thought could possibly be necessary, well before you go round a left hand corner. On the way round, you find a queue stopped ahead of you. As he draws serenely, safely, to a halt, you wonder, "how did he know the queue was there?". The answer was that Jack earlier noticed brakelights from the back of the queue, being reflected in the side panels of the last car which went by the other way. He knew there was a reason for stopping before he could see what it was; and he took no chance.

The advanced driver signals in good time, and is *always in the correct position* for any manoeuvre that he or she is about to make. In town traffic we find that Jill does not swing wildly from one lane to another. She "noses over" to another lane of traffic, if necessary, a long way before she needs to, so that she never deprives anyone of their rightful position, or makes them slow down. By taking in the extra long view ahead, as well as the near view, Jill avoids the last-second panics which beset the novice.

Jack is aware that most "shunts" are caused by traffic following each other too close and by drivers failing to anticipate that a knot of cars ahead is stopping. He follows at three or four times the usual gap on wet roads and by up to ten times the gap in fog, or even more on ice or snow.

Directly he sees any "problem" far ahead, he touches his

brakes so as to flick on the brakelights. This warns those following of possible danger. In heavy fog or snow, if he has to stop, he keeps his brakelights on...

If an accident were ever to be unavoidable, he would always choose the lesser of evils. For example, he would always try to avoid a head-on smash, but might have to make an exception, were the only alternative to be to run into a crowd of bystanders.

At closing time Jill is on the look-out for drunks, both the self-destruct kind (pedestrians), who may fall over into the road in front of her, and the lethal kind in cars. She gives all potentially incapacitated pedestrians a wide berth.

She keeps in mind whether the school holidays are on; in term, if it is the time of day children travel to, and come out of, school, she will be especially aware of the sorts of places from which kiddies can come pelting out.

Burst Tyres And Punctures

A new tyre may burst unexpectedly, though it is rare. They should be "run in" for 100 miles or so, so that you can be sure the tyre beads have bedded in properly around the wheel rim. Other causes for a burst tyre may be under-inflation, which damages its walls through the heat created by undue flexing, and *developing* damage, sustained after hitting a kerb.

If a kerb is touched at speed the tyre must be looked over by an expert, even if there has not been an accident. The steering must also be checked for its proper alignment. The same attention is demanded if a kerb is biffed severely during parking, such is the danger.

A sudden "blow out" may cause the car to lurch to one side or the other. The extent would depend on speed and whether you were perhaps cornering or braking at the time, either of which could accentuate your problems. A rear tyre burst can be as dangerous in this respect as a front one.

The best advice for a front or rear burst is to hold firmly on the steering wheel so as to counteract any skewing round, and to try to let the car run safely to a standstill. Do not jam on the brakes. You may get away with some light, progressive braking but even most of that may have to be abandoned if it is pulling you wildly off course. If traffic conditions demand a quicker stop, you must try your best.

The sign of a puncture may be wandering steering, or a "heavy" action to it. You may become aware of a "thumping", apparently coming from the suspension. Or, the first thing you may notice, could be slewing round as you try to brake, just as with a burst tyre. Hopefully you will spot a puncture way before then. At the first sign, stop and check your tyres. Punctures are more common in wet weather, when the water lubricates the path of foreign objects through the rubber.

Flood Water

Passing through deep water, such as at a ford, brake linings can get saturated. Older cars with drum brakes are affected more seriously than ones with disc brakes. Until the water has been "steamed" off, by applying the brakes on the move, you have almost no stopping power at your command. If this happens, drive slowly (up to 10 m.p.h.) while braking gently to dry the linings. As little as 20-30 metres should be enough to clear the water.

Night Driving

Although I am dealing with night driving in this "After Your Test" part of the book, most learners, as they approach the Test and become more confident, can begin night driving once their instructor is also happy that they are up to it.

The constant message at night is to *contain speed below that from which you can stop safely, well within the lit area of your headlights.*

As soon as lighting-up time arrives, put on your headlights. On "dark" days it may also be worth having a few minutes on sidelights alone, beforehand. Although it is permissible where there is good street lighting (as defined by law), to continue on sidelights alone after "official" darkness, I strongly recommend you to use headlights always – to be seen, not just to see. On a badly lit road – as so many are anyway – it's madness to leave them off.

There is no need to be dazzled from behind. Switch your interior mirror to the night-dim position, or adjust the mirror slightly, so that reflections do not "burn" directly into your eyes. However, you need to be aware that on night dim setting, your interior mirror will distort distances considerably.

The basic rule is to keep headlights dipped whenever someone is coming the other way (even a cyclist), or whenever there is anyone in front of you who might be dazzled via his or her mirrors . However, you must discipline yourself to **use high beam at all other night times.** It is essential to see to the best advantage, *and to be seen coming* at the earliest possible moment.

Because "up" headlight beams penetrate the far distance, anyone there gets an early warning of your approach that is denied them by the permanently dipped motorist. This tell-tale warning often saves a life.

Using "up" beam also helps anyone intending to overtake to see when to go. Dip once they pass, 'til they are out of beam range ahead.

Several up and down "flashes", as you approach a dark country junction, where yours is the major road and no-one is coming the other way, constitute a superb, silent, night horn, with which to alert anyone on the minor road(s).

While dipped for approaching traffic, avoid being dazzled by them, by concentrating your view on the road in front on your side, which is being lit by your own lights. Apart from noting that they are well over on their side of the road, never look directly at oncoming headlights. Certainly never gaze at them; you cannot be hypnotised (by lights) unless you allow it!

At dark unlit junctions looking right, left, and right again, needs more time. Time for slow sweeping looks, which will pick up from the shadows, those unlit skateboards, horses, or other surprising dangers which fool drivers who take insufficent care.

Overtaking At Night
On two-way roads, extra hazards arise with the difficulty of assessing the speed of approaching traffic. Most drivers probably do this subconsciously, allowing themselves extra time to form their judgment, and relating what they see to previous experience of seeing headlights getting nearer. This does not, however, work so well when the approaching vehicle is a motorcylist, or a lorry or car driving *illegally* on a single headlight. Also, certain vehicles such as jeeps, have the headlights close together, so they look further away than they are.

Another problem is the driver in front who, on a straight, clear road, remains on dipped headlights. Such drivers are as much a menace to themselves, as they are to you.

Your problem is to see how far ahead the road is clear. You have to move out at a safe moment so that you can flash your headlights up for a second and look well past. Be ready to accelerate or drop back, depending what you see. Also be watchful that this sort of driver does not get dazzled in his or her mirrors, and panic. You must not intentionally dazzle someone.

In one sense, overtaking at night is a little safer, in that you can see the *beam* of an approaching car's headlights before you can see the lights. But do not imagine you can overtake just because there are no lights. There might be drunken wanderers, animals, a bend, anything. Pick out the road in your own lights and drive only as fast as you can see it is safe and clear to do.

Any of these last hazards can be lurking on a dual carriageway or a motorway too! Such roads do not provide an excuse for speeds above your light-power.

Skidding

Aquaplaning, a deadly type of skid, was explained on page 171. It can happen on any fast road. The fine skins of water ("ponds") which were mentioned, are commonly experienced out in the country where drainage is less efficient. At night, when you have little warning because they're not so easy to see, they can be lethal. Control your speed! Acceleration, cornering and braking are dependent on the grip between your tyres and the road.

Exceed the grip possible and you will skid:

1. If you are *over-accelerating,* the driven wheels will spin faster than they can propel you. The car may slide sideways at the driven wheels as well.
2. If you are *braking too hard,* one or more wheels will lock (stop turning) and slide on, carried by the car's momentum (weight x speed). You may also be thrown off course, or, ultimately, into a spin; see pages 35 and 186.
3. If you are *cornering too fast* altogether, and simply exceed the grip holding you to the steered course, you slide out, off the corner, carried both by momentum and centrifugal force.

If you *over-*accelerate ON A CORNER OR A BEND, or, alternatively, brake too much, cornering grip is more easily beaten. Either of these is therefore a big mistake. Before I can guide you towards safest cornering (page 186), I must explain the root causes of skidding.

Grip is affected by the weight and design of your vehicle, its speed, and the circumstances. Momentum and centrifugal force are increased by extra weight or higher speed. But of greater importance are the conditions of your tyre treads (which *must* be good by law, see page 11), and of the road surface (which may be good, or, *awful*). You must constantly take into account changing road surfaces.

Really appalling surfaces include: loose gravel, wet leaves (you slide on the leaves or stones without touching the tarmac), damp cobblestones, oil patches, and wet mud. But ordinary roads vary enormously. One is old, and treacherous because the surface has been highly polished by the traffic. Another is new and comparatively "tacky". Residential streets are built to less exacting standards than major roads. Many country roads dip towards their outside edges at bends, instead of having the camber, as it is known, engineered to do the opposite, and rise. That would lessen your chance of skidding, whereas adverse cambers actually increase it, drastically.

Wetness makes any surface dramatically worse. The initial dampness when rain falls may be the most slippery of all, before oiliness and dust have washed away, but soaking wet roads are still a big skid risk. In wet, you should always be down to around ⅔ of dry road speeds, at the most.

Ice, black ice, snow, and freezing rain, all discussed later, may be ten times worse. Possible grip becomes almost non-existent.

Best Action When You Skid

You may have heard the expression "steer into a skid". The concept can apply to all 1-3 types of skid above. The object is to counteract, at once, any loss of steering direction. If the back of the car has begun to swing to one side, you have to steer in a flash the same way that the back is sliding – that is, "into the skid". If a slide starts at the front, again, steer towards where the car has begun to go, but all you need is to get the front wheels as straight as you can, instantly. This quick action with the steering has to be done within a trice but not overdone. Immediately some semblance of steering control is restored, keep things as straight as you can, unless forced to try to avoid hitting whoever or whatever may be in your path.

It isn't only steering correction you may have to be quick with. Refer again to skids, 1, 2, 3 above:

1. *You gave too much acceleration – one or more driving wheels are spinning:*

reduce acceleration instantly, but only long enough to stop the spinning; correct steering fast, just enough, no more; accelerate again **straightaway,** but **gently** this time.

You must have some re-acceleration, because that small "driving" force is needed to help the steering take the car out of trouble. (Note: if you are in the midst of a bend when you start to skid like this, a complete lift-off of your accelerator pedal could serve to worsen it. It is better, if possible, before you resume that gentle re-acceleration, not to lift off to such an extent that you are ever on "over-run", i.e. driven wheels pushing engine instead of vice versa).

2. *You are braking too hard and a wheel(s) lock(s):*

reduce your footbrake pressure fast, not right off, just enough to let the wheel(s) roll again; instantly restore that pressure, but only as near as you dare to the "locking point"; if she locks again, repeat. This was all gone into in greater detail in Chapter 3.

3. *You went too fast into a bend, and now the car is skidding straight on instead of going round:*

this must never be allowed to happen as it is usually impossible to extricate yourself before it is too late. There may be slight hope if: (a) *over*-acceleration going into the bend has caused a driving wheel wheel-spin, or (b) braking on the corner has caused a wheel or wheels to lock.

In (a) follow the advice given under **1**, just above, exactly. Slashing acceleration by the right amount, *and no more,* may give you the chance to steer to safety, as you gently keep the car driven by the accelerator (i.e. just clear of over-run). In (b) get *some* of the pressure off the brake (as just explained in **2**), so as to grab any slender chance to steer for safety.

The overall balance of the car is a key factor in relation to cornering skids. Centrifugal force is placing most of the car's weight on the outer two wheels and, at the same time, lifting it off the inner two. That weight, if you are to give each outside wheel its best chance of gripping, must therefore be made to fall on both of them as equally as possible.

During braking, weight is thrown forwards; under acceleration it is thrown back. You can see the car's nose dip under braking, and, conversely, the front rise during acceleration. This helps explain why, given the need to equalise the weight going to each of the two outside wheels as far as possible, you must neither brake (except gently), nor *over*-accelerate on a corner.

If you do brake excessively on a bend, too much weight all goes on to the front outside wheel. Its possible grip may be beaten. This can happen even if it doesn't quite lock. Because the load is mainly *off* all the other wheels, including the back outside one, they are not much help in restraining the skid which may develop.

If, the on the other hand, you *over*-accelerate on a corner, some weight tends to come off the outside front wheel, reducing its grip. It may then slide, carrying the other (also lightened) front wheel along with it. Wheel-spin, on a front-wheel-drive car, may even promote the slide.

Although *over*-acceleration on a bend transfers a fair degree of weight onto the back outside wheel, on a rear-wheel-drive car it can still cause rear wheel-spin there, which then promotes the back of the car to slide off the corner.

"Breakaway" at the back like this can be sudden and very vicious. Unless the front breaks away first (in which event the entire car will want to slide on forwards and possibly clean off the road), you may find yourself – if you are not quick enough to lighten your foot on the accelerator, as well as then restore it by just the right amount – in an almost instantaneous spin. That I deal with, further below.

Meanwhile, I can touch briefly on oversteer and understeer, terms of which you may have heard. To avoid the horror of a complete spin, set off as just described, all cars are designed with a tendency to understeer. This characteristic causes the front wheels to turn the car on a fractionally wider arc than steered. It will also normally ensure, if sharp cornering is ever indulged in at excessive speed, that the front wheels will lose their grip, and hence slide, before the back ones. A front wheel-skid, bad as it is, is usually easier to get out of than sudden breakaway at the back.

In an oversteering car, the back would always want to go first, taking you round with it... Even in a four wheel slide such as was suggested above, taking your entire car towards the ditch, you probably have a greater chance of regaining control and saving yourself, than when (in a rear-wheel-drive car), total rear-end breakaway has got you in its grip.

Fortunately, most drivers first experience the skidding effects of over-acceleration when trying to get away from a standing start too fast, rather than when stupidly trying to *over-power* their way round a bend. What to do, given in **1** above, is learned first-hand but in the comparative safety of slow overall speed. An experienced instructor should easily be able to demonstrate take-off wheel-spin in perfect safety, on a wet day, so that you can see what happens and learn exactly how to handle it.

Safest Cornering

The safest method of cornering is based on understanding balance and skidding from all the above.

YOU MUST DO ALL NECESSARY SLOWING DOWN, VIA CHANGING DOWN THE GEARS AND BRAKING (if any), BEFORE A CORNER OR A BEND IS REACHED.

Get speed down to *below* that which you know from experience will be O.K. for normal steering grip to work. You can then "drive" round with slight acceleration – acceleration which you should be able to "feel" setting the car on course nicely, and for which you should already be in the right gear. The car will go round with its weight evenly distributed and mainly on the outside wheels.

Suppose the worst happens. You skid into a spin, through 180° or more. Keep cool! There will (if you haven't yet hit something) probably come a point where with a bit of help from the steering, the car will start to run off its spinning axis, and straight backwards (or maybe it will be forwards!). At that stage, if you get your brakes on again quickly, you may avoid piling into a hedge or whatever. Then you may need more quick-thinking. Suppose you were now in the middle lane of a motorway and facing the **wrong** way? You would get your headlights on so as to ensure everyone spotted your plight, whilst you swung round as safely as possible to face the right way on the hard shoulder. I'll stick with this one example; the point is, whatever the circumstances may be, keep your brain switched on at least 'til all avenues are tried.

Ice And Snow

These conditions dictate a maximum sane speed of 20 m.p.h. – most of the time it must be slower.

"Black" (invisible) ice is a death trap because of the surprise element. In freezing weather be on the look-out for it at open windswept places. Be warned by a sudden light feeling in the steering, by any minor skid, or by seeing everyone going slowly. Motorbikes will be the first to give you this clue; they're closest to the (thin) ice! The same skidding control techniques all apply to ice, only everything is ten times more slippery! Freezing rain is even worse.

Snow gets packed down and becomes like ice. Neither are recommended for driving on 'til you have two or three years' qualified experience. Pick crunchy fresh areas of snow for better grip, if possible.

On snow and/or ice, to get up hills, and to get away from standing should you get stuck, you must always use the *highest* possible gear, combined with the absolute minimum of acceleration. If it is only a slight hill, try starting in 3rd or 2nd. (On the level you might even be able to get moving in top when no other gear will get you going.) This reduces the chance of wheel-spin at the driven wheels, which can defeat your getting away. Going uphill, take the highest gear you reckon that you can get away with, before you start the ascent. Changing down on the way up may be impossible without wheel-spin setting in when you come to release the clutch to try to take up the drive in the lower gear.

Rather than ever having to stop on an uphill gradient, watch the traffic progress ahead of you and be canny; wait on the level 'til you can see you can go all the way up the hill without needing a stop. If you time things carefully at junctions, you may be able to avoid stops at them too. Equally, if you are cagey, you can sometimes choose the best places to stop when traffic is having to queue.

Once a wheel spins, you may well get "dug" in and stuck. The best hope then is usually to reverse, if safe to do so, so you can try again off "unspun" snow (or ice); otherwise try "rocking" yourself out by means of alternate back and forwards attempts. If neither works, you will need a push. Surprisingly (because no-one ever seems to think of it) a push generally works best with the engine off. Flailing wheels and a high-revving engine serve mainly to burn rubber off your tyres; they get you out hardly at all.

Get into low gear at the top, before going down any snowy or icy hill. Hold speed at barely moving, at least until you find it may be safe to go a little faster, or you will swiftly find yourself skidding down out of control. Fresh snow will hold you back better than packed down, iced-up snow, so find that if you can.

If you are in any doubt about whether a steep and icy hill may be safe to attempt to descend at all, one of the finest driving techniques you can fall back on is to watch someone else go first... Let their experience be your guide but never encourage...

It is almost no use thinking in terms of braking distances to follow behind people on snow and ice. You can't measure them! What you must do instead, is continually make small tests, very lightly, on the brakes, to establish how much braking power you actually have at the moment. That is to say *before you need it.*

Way out, before you reach any junction or place that you must stop, discover what your stopping power is likely to be, in much the same way, *before* it is too late.

Brake Failure

Be warned if your brake pedal needs pushing down further than usual before it acts. Loss of hydraulic brake fluid is the likely cause and the trouble can worsen rapidly. If "pumping" the pedal improves the situation, the fault has already reached serious proportions; a dashboard warning light may confirm your suspicions but don't let lack of one deter you from stopping to check the fluid reservoir itself, immediately.

Sudden total brake failure is, thankfully, unusual. Quick action may avert a smash. Pump the footbrake; it may still help a bit. "Crash" down the gears to 1st, for engine resistance braking, as well as using the handbrake. Hoot your horn and flash your lights to warn people. Look for any safe refuge to run off the road. If all is lost anyway, choose the least damaging thing to hit; certainly try to avoid a head-on accident.

A Final Word

The art of driving is always so to adjust your speed and position, in relation to road conditions and to other road users, **and in anticipation of them,** that you rarely, if ever, land in trouble. Do that, and avoid over-confidence, and so long as lady luck remains on your side, you should stay safe.

My editorial team and I, are right behind you when you take your Test, ready to help, wishing you luck. Behind this book's Guarantee stands an added bonus. Provided you send a stamped, self-addressed envelope we will, free of charge, as fast as we can, advise on any driving problem. It is part of our commitment to road safety.

INDEX

A

Acceleration, 43, 50, 85
Accelerator, 16, 22 et seq.
   during skidding, 172, 182 et seq.
   when changing gear, 45
Accidents, 29, 36, 49, 60 et. seq.
   , action in event of, 154, 160, 164
   and the law, 67, 106, 154
   , avoidable, 81, 102, 112, 116,
      120, 126, 127, 164
   , causes, 29, 58, 65, 75, 76, 78, 80,
      83, 102, 117, 160, 161
   , motorway, 171 et seq., 177
Advanced driving, 178 et seq.
Anticipation, 29, 31, 36, 37, 51, 55,
   60, 65, 77, 80, 86, 96, 101, 105,
   126, 127, 129, 178, 179
Anti-lock brakes, 36, 164
Aquaplaning, 171
Arrows, on road, 97
Automatic transmission, 15, 67, 141, 144

B

Bends, 55, 56, 102, 155, 163, 184, 185
Blind people, 64
   spot, 12, 89, 140
Box junctions, 61, 116
Brake failure, 12, 28, 31, 188
   , foot, 15, 16, 28, 29
   , hand, 15, 22, 28, 29, 93, 188
   lights, 30, 156, 165
   linings, 46, 180
Brakes, defective, 67, 180, 188
Braking and skidding, 182 et seq.
   anti-lock, 36, 164
   at bends, 182
   , engine, 34, 44 et seq., 188
   , familiarisation, 16, 28, 30, 33, 35
   in emergency, 14, 25, 31 et seq.,
      179, 180
   , locked wheel, 32, 35, 182, 184
   on motorways, 177
   on snow and ice, 187
   unnecessarily, 152
   , what happens, 28-30, 32 et seq.
Breakdowns, 67, 141, 154, 173, 174
Bus lanes, 128, 156, 165

C

Camber, 183
Car, mechanical condition, 12
   tax, 67
   width, 38, 56

"Cat's eyes", 155, 157, 163
Children, 13 et seq.
Choke, 17 et seq., 81
Clearance (see Distance)
Clearways, 155, 162
Clutch control, 14 et seq., 16, 19 et seq.,
   22 et seq., 29, 89, 133, 134
   , slipping the, 19 et seq., 25, 50,
      133, 134, 138
   wear, 25, 37, 50
   when changing gear, 45
      stopping, 29, 37
Coasting, 50
Contra-flows, 176
Corner control, 56, 85, 94, 95, 101, 124
Cornering, safest, 186
   too fast, 182
"Countdown markers", 174
Courtesy, 53, 60, 63, 66, 77, 98, 152
Cutting in, 120
Cycle lanes, 155, 162
Cyclists, 85, 106, 110, 129, 160, 161

D

Disqualification, 67
Distances, clearance from vehicles, 53, 78
   , following, 35, 118, 155, 161, 162
   from kerb, 38, 53, 89, 104, 132 et seq.,
   , stopping, 35, 61
      behind vehicles, 161
   when overtaking, 119, 126
Door opening, 67, 78, 154
Double white line, 67, 97, 126, 154
Drink-driving, 67, 152, 155, 163
Driver, legal responsibilities, 12, 14
Dual carriageway, joining, 156, 165
   , turns, 97, 98, 102 et seq.

E

Emergency stop, 31 et seq., 36
Engine braking, 34, 44 et seq., 188
   , flooding, 18
   , idling, 22, 147
   pulling power, 46
   , starting, 14 et seq., 18, 25
   , switching off, 18
Eyesight, 67

F

First aid, 156, 160, 165
Fog, 57, 102, 154, 156, 161, 165, 172
Fuel, 13, 174, 175

INDEX

G

Gap, (see Distance and Overtaking)
Gears, at roundabouts, 114
, changing, 14 *et seq.*, 22, 23, 41, 42
et. seq., 46, 47, 50, 186, 188
, clutch routine, 45, 48
, 5th, 42, 50
for left turns, 85 *et seq.*
overtaking, 119 *et seq.*
right turns, 90 *et seq.*
in snow and ice, 187
in traffic, 44, 46 *et seq.*

H

Hard shoulder, 141, 162, 173, 176
Hatch road markings, 96, 97
Hazard warning lights, 68
Headlights, 154, 156, 164, 180, 181,
, dazzling, 13, 180 *et seq.*
, dipping, 13, 15, 180, 181
flasher, 57, 70, 101, 181, 188
, high beam, 180, 181
in daytime, 16
Heater, 15, 172
Hesitation, 49, 84, 152
Highway Code, 68, 149, 156
Hills, 27, 47, 49, 61, 97, 124
in snow and ice, 187
on motorways, 177
Horn, 13, 156

I

Ice, 161, 186 *et seq.*
Ignition switch, 18
Indicators, 15
at junctions, 82 *et seq.*
, difficult to see, 68
, failure, 67, 68
to cancel, 70, 75, 82
on motorways, 173, 174
, timing, 70
Information, further, 2, 188
Insurance, 12, 14, 60, 67, 154

J

Junctions, 48, 61, 156, 165, 181
, going straight on, 72, 73, 106
, handbrake/gear routine, 37, 85, 93
, observation at, 82 *et seq.*, 102, 152
, turning left, 85 *et seq.*
right, 90 *et seq.*

L

Lane changing, 51, 55, 65, 106, 124
, dual carriageways, 102, 110
for temporary advantage, 128
, one ways, 104, 105
, overtaking, 117 *et seq.*
, roundabouts, 108 *et seq.*
on motorways, 171, 175, 176
, bus, 128, 156, 160, 165

, cycle, 155, 160, 162
discipline, 55, 69, 102 *et seq.*,
127, 156, 165
, indiscipline, 152
markings, 55, 125, 154, 162, 163
Level crossings, 154, 156, 159, 164
Licence, 7, 11, 14, 15, 67, 149, 154
Lights, brakelights, 30, 74, 75, 80
, dashboard warning, 13, 177, 188
, headlights (see Headlights)
, hazard warning, 68
, motorway warning, 173
, sidelights, 180
Loads, 13, 155, 162

M

M.O.T. certificate, 67, 154
Mirrors, 29-30, 175
adjustment, 12, 180
after a turn, 70, 85, 111
blind spots, 31, 121, 175
, how to use, 29, 122, 154
, insufficient use, 66
, moving off, 78
on motorways, 122, 171 *et seq.*
, overtaking, 119 *et seq.*
routine, 51
, turning left, 85 *et seq.*
right, 90 *et seq.*
Motorcycle, 98, 106, 109, 120, 122, 129
Motorways, 153, 171 *et seq.*
Moving off, 22 *et seq.*, 77 *et seq.*,
downhill, 27
on a steep hill, 27
, running back, 27, 49
Mud on road, 183
shoes, 14

N

Neutral, 16, 21
Night driving, 77, 85, 102, 153, 154,
164, 180 *et seq.*

O

Observation, 14, 16, 22, 23, 39, 51, 56,
60, 65
at junctions, 82 *et seq.*, 102, 104,
124, 152
night, 181
roundabouts, 108 *et seq.*, 116
traffic lights, 106 *et seq.*
during manoeuvres, 131 *et seq.*
for overtaking, 118 *et seq.*
in emergencies, 29, 30
of parked vehicles, 79, 80
pedestrians, 82, 84
two wheeled traffic, 82, 109
on motorways, 176, 177
snow and ice, 187
when moving off, 78
parking, 143

INDEX

Obstruction, 55, 61, 67, 75, 141, 159
, moving, 127, 158
Offences, 66, 173, 176
One ways, 104, 105, 128, 152
Overtaking, 50, 51, 60, 103, 117
anticipation ahead, 126
at night, 181
, clearance from overtaken vehicle,
119, 126
dangerously, 85, 86, 126
errors, 122 *et seq.*
, exposure to danger, 117 *et seq.*
, gap, 117, 124, 127, 157
in one-way street, 105
, mirrors, 119
on dual carriageway, 103, 112, 127
motorways, 171, 174, 175
nearside or inside, 91, 94, 104,
105, 112, 114, 128, 129
, ready position, 118
signals, 117
slow-moving vehicles, 155, 162
speed, 118 *et seq.*
, three lane two-way road, 125, 157
, timing, 118 *et seq.*
, warning toot, 127
, when not to, 117, 124

P
Parking, 38, 60, 67, 75, 141 *et seq.*,
153 *et seq.*
Pavement, 88, 89, 159
Pedestrian crossings, 37, 49
, pelican crossings, 64
queuing at, 64
, right of way, 58, 62 *et seq.*, 85
et seq., 158, 159
stopping/handbrake/gear routine, 37,
63
, zebra crossings, 49, 58, 63
Positioning, 51
at roundabouts, 108 *et seq.*
, bad, 152
by others, 101, 112, 114
, "crown of the road", 90
for bends, 56
left turn, 69, 84, 87, 89
overtaking, 117 *et seq.*
right turn, 90, *et seq.*, 124
in one-way street, 104
to pass parked vehicle, 76
Practice, 8, 9
Pulling in, 30, 38, 75, 155, 164
Puncture, 52, 155, 162, 179

Q
Questions on Test, 135, 141, 152, 153
Queues, 38, 48, 50, 64, 106, 116, 128,
155, 187

R
Reversing, 41, 66, 130 *et seq.*, 152
on Test, Golden Rules, 140
round a corner, 75, 135-136, 152
Right of way, 7, 53, 58 *et seq.*
along major road, 61, 81, 93
at junctions, 81, 93, 155, 163
in reverse, 66, 130, 139
, overtaking, 117 *et seq.*
, roundabouts, 108 *et seq.*
Road conditions, bad, 162, 183, 186
hog, 53
Roadworks, 56, 65, 106, 176
Roundabouts, 65, 69, 105 *et seq.*
, handbrake/gear routine, 114
, left, 110
, "mini", 108
, right, 112
, straight on, 110
, timing, 116
Rules of the road, 60 *et seq.*
at box junctions, 62
junctions, 61, 80 *et seq.*
roundabouts, 65, 108 *et seq.*
traffic lights, 62
, correct path at crossroads, 97 *et seq.*
for obstructions, 61
non-drivers, 153
pedestrians, 37, 58 *et seq.*,
62 *et seq.*, 80, 106, 108 *et
seq.*, 158, 159, 161
, giving way at parked vehicle,
53, 59, 76, 77
, if involved in accident, 154
on narrow roads, 60
, overtaking, 117 *et seq.*
on inside, 128
, precedence at junctions, 91, 92,
93, 101, 102, 103
, three lane, two-way road, 125, 157
, times when the law says stop, 154
, to drive on left, 52, 60, 152, 157
when changing lane, 65
overtaken, 118, 122, 153
reversing, 66
where approaching vehicle has
priority, 154
, which lane?, 157

S
School crossing patrol, 63, 67, 107
Seat, 12, 13
Signals, 68 *et seq.*
, arm, 30, 41, 69, 72 *et seq.*
, how to give, etc., 35 *et
seq.*, 154
at roundabouts, 69, 109 *et seq.*
before reversing, 77, 136
by others, 128, 153
, difficult to see, 69

Signals (continued)
   for lane change, 65, 129
   , inadequate, 152
   , left, 69, 73, 85 *et seq.*
   , misinterpretation, 57, 70, 77, 82,
      101, 127
   , moving off, 73, 77, 78
   , overtaking, 117 *et seq.*, 126
   , passing parked vehicle, 60, 76, 77
   , pulling in, 38, 73, 75, 77
   , slowing down, 30, 73 *et seq.*
   , straight ahead, 72, 73
   , timing, 70, 72 *et seq.*, 78, 94
   to police etc., 72, 73
Signs, filter arrow, 53, 155, 162, 163
   , give-way, 61
   , instructional (blue), 155, 162
   , mandatory, 67, 163
   , shape of, 155, 163
   , stop, 61
   , warning, 155, 162, 163, 173, 176
      177
Single track road, 60
Skidding, 31, 32, 35, 171, 182 *et seq.*
   , "steering into a skid", 183
"Slip roads", 173
Slipping the clutch, 19 *et seq.*, 25,
   50, 133, 134, 138
"Snail's pace", 25, 53, 133, 134
Snow, 57, 161, 186 *et seq.*
Speed, 51, 53, 61, 176
   approaching junction with minor road,
      81, 82, 89
   at bends, 55
      night, 154, 180 *et seq.*
   control during danger, 80, 103, 154
   , dangerous, 66, 172
   downhill, 46
   , driving fast, 128, 175, 176
      very slowly, 25, 26
   joining major road, 89
   , judgment of on motorways, 172 *et
      seq.*, 176
   limit, 55, 103, 155, 156, 163, 164,
      on motorways, 164, 173, 175, 176
   on ice and snow, 186
      narrow lanes, 60
   , overtaking, 118
   , passing parked vehicle(s), 79
   , too slow, 85
   ,   fast, 89
   unsuited to conditions, 152
   , uphill, 46
Speedometer, 12, 44, 51, 176
Stalling, 18, 25, 26, 29, 31, 34, 48,
   81, 83, 93, 147, 154
Steering, 39 *et seq.*
   at junctions, 89, 93
   check, 179
   during a skid, 183 *et seq.*
   in reverse, 130 *et seq.*
   , loss of, 32 *et seq.*, 36, 172
   , mechanical fault, 67
   on icy roads, 186
   , self-centring, 40
   technique, 40, 74
   , tyre burst, 179, 180

T
Tail-gating, 123
Test (Driving), 89, 95, 97, 100, 148
   et seq.
   manoeuvres, 130 *et seq.*
   requirements, 17, 23, 27, 31, 39,
      40, 61, 148, 149
"Three-point-turn", 132 *et seq.*, 152
Tiredness, 8, 11, 162
Traffic, 15
   during manoeuvres, 132, 133, 136,
      137
   flow, 55
   , gears in, 44, 46 *et seq.*
   jams, moving, 161
   lights, 62, 67, 105 *et seq.*
      at roadworks, 106
      , filter arrow, 53, 128, 154
      , handbrake gear routine, 160
   , safe following distance, 155, 161
   sequence, 154
   , slow-moving, 56
Tyre grip, 32, 182, 183
   law, 11
   pressure, 11, 172, 179
Tyres, burst and punctures, 179
   damage to, 38, 52, 179
   , defective, 11, 67

U
U-turn, 135, 155, 163

V
Visibility, 57, 161, 180, 181

W
Warning signs, 155, 163
      on motorways, 162, 173, 176,
      177
   triangle, 67, 142
Wheel lock, 133
Whiplash, 38
Windows, 12 *et seq.*, 89
Windscreen, smashed, 126
   washers, 12, 13, 15
   wipers, 13, 15, 172

Z
Zebra crossing, 49, 58, 63, 155